If Ministers Fall, Can They Be Restored?

OTHER BOOKS BY TIM LAHAYE

How to Win Over Depression
Revelation: Illustrated and Made Plain
Sex Education Is for the Family
The Act of Marriage (with Beverly LaHaye)
Anger Is a Choice (with Bob Phillips)
Finding the Will of God in a Crazy, Mixed-Up World

If Ministers Fall, Can They Be Restored?

Tim LaHaye

PYRANEE
BOOKS

Zondervan Publishing House
Grand Rapids, Michigan

If Ministers Fall, Can They Be Restored?
Copyright © 1990 by Tim LaHaye

A Pyranee Book
Published by the Zondervan Publishing House
1415 Lake Drive, S.E., Grand Rapids, Michigan 49506

Library of Congress Cataloging-in-Publication Data

LaHaye, Tim F.
    If ministers fall, can they be restored? / Tim LaHaye.
      p. cm.
    ISBN 0-310-52131-9
    1. Clergy—Sexual behavior. 2. Clergy—Deposition.
    3. Evangelicism—United States. I. Title.
    BV4392.L34   1990
    253'.2—dc20   90–31066
                                          CIP

All Scripture quotations, unless otherwise noted, are taken from the HOLY BIBLE: NEW INTERNATIONAL VERSION (North American Edition). Copyright © 1973, 1978, 1984 by the International Bible Society. Used by permission of Zondervan Bible Publishers.

Printed in the United States of America

90 91 92 93 94 95 / AK / 10 9 8 7 6 5 4 3 2 1

*This book is dedicated to
my wife, Beverly,
the best friend I have on earth,
whose life and love have been a
constant source of fulfillment that has
given real purpose and meaning to my
life for over forty wonderful years.
Because of her I could write this book.*

CONTENTS

Part I
If Ministers Fall ...

CHAPTER *1*

What On Earth Is Going On in the Church?

*T*wo years ago a woman on an American Airlines flight from San Francisco to Dallas was seated next to a young, bearded man. Noticing that he refused the offer of a meal, she asked, "Are you not feeling well?"

"No," he replied, "this is my day for prayer and fasting." Assuming that he was a Christian, she identified herself as a believer and asked if he had accepted Christ. She wasn't ready for his response.

"No, I am a Satanist." He then explained that leaders of the Satanist church had designated every Tuesday as "a day of prayer and fasting that the homes and marriages of Christian ministers throughout America would be destroyed." Then he added, "Several of us are concentrating on the ministers of Dallas, Texas."

Whether or not the man's prayers to Satan had any effect, who can deny that moral infidelity has struck ministers' marriages like a plague, bringing respect for ministers of the gospel to an all-time low? You have doubtless heard of the well-publicized televangelist sex scandals, which the media delight in bringing to the attention of the entire country. Seldom mentioning the vast majority of ministers who have faithfully kept their wedding vows, the media love to heap discredit on all Christian leaders for the transgressions of a few.

I find the woman's narrative quite startling because I am familiar with the target city of Dallas. And for the past five years the city has been rocked by one moral tragedy after another—and the people who received the most media coverage were ministers.

One well-publicized case involved a minister who fell in love with a female psychologist in the congregation. As the story unfolded, the media reported that the minister's wife had been attacked in her home and choked. Although the wife lived, she remains at this writing in a comatose state, unable to care for their two small children. The minister, who was relieved of his pastorate, remains the chief suspect, but as yet the authorities haven't gathered enough details to file charges. According to the latest press reports, the minister is living in San Francisco with the psychologist.

One dynamic, young minister was sent to jail for violent rape charges—of ten different women. Naturally, this story hit the front page of every newspaper in the city.

After teaching a Bible class one Sunday morning in Dallas, I preached for a young minister in a nearby church and was extremely impressed with his dynamic challenge to a growing congregation. After meeting his wife and three children, I thought, "What a beautiful family." On the following Wednesday night the deacons confronted the pastor with reports they chose to keep silent; the next day the minister and his family vacated the parsonage and vanished.

The associate pastor of another congregation called my office, seeking advice. A member of the congregation had discovered that his own wife had been having an affair with the senior pastor. The elders needed help in handling the situation.

Dallas Magazine, the popular, muckraking monthly that delights in exposing the hypocrisy of Christians—particularly ministers—devoted its September 1988 issue to an unbelievably depraved accusation against a young minister of a growing Baptist church in North Dallas. The minister was accused by his church leaders of having affairs with seven women in the congregation, including one divorced woman who claimed many affairs with him over a four-year period. The minister was also accused of "lying, seduction, harassment, and greed." Even though the minister was arrested by the police for stealing condoms from a store, was under investigation by the IRS, and was accused of embezzlement, he continued to preach in his church for another eight months before resigning in disgrace.[1]

In another case a minister's wife of twenty-five years left him for a married man in the congregation. It not only destroyed his marriage but also ruined his ministry. Today he is a salesman.

A brokenhearted father, graduate of a Bible college where he met "his dedicated Christian wife," sobbed out the story of his wife leaving him and their two children for a man in their church—who abandoned his wife with four children.

Then another tragic case hit the press: the pastor of one of the fastest-growing churches in the nation resigned suddenly for "moral indiscretion." The entire denomination was stunned and saddened.

But Dallas doesn't have a corner on the sin of adultery. Within the last year and a half, twelve ministers I know personally have fallen sexually.

Furthermore, ministerial infidelity is by no means limited to liberal churches. One pastor of a conservative denomination widely respected for its high standards of godly living was found guilty by a jury of "misconduct through therapeutic deception while knowing" that the female counselee "was emotionally dependent on him." According to the January 1989 report of the International

Religious News Service, this pastor was the first minister convicted under a 1986 law forbidding sexual exploitation by therapists and clergy. Following months of meeting together, he and the woman left town and apparently lived together for three months. Each left a spouse and three children behind, but the woman later returned to her family. The former minister, now a used car salesman, is still estranged from his family. The woman has filed a $250,000 civil suit against him, the church, the denomination, and denominational officials.

Not even seasoned ministers are immune from the tangled web of infidelity. I recently learned of a seventy-year-old counseling pastor, a foreign missionary for many years, who was having affairs with two different women in his congregation at the same time.

Obviously something is seriously wrong in the church. Some people would say that every generation has seen its ministers fall into sexual sin, that it is just more advertised today. While there is no doubt that many of the media use every opportunity to discredit the Christian community, it does seem that ministerial infidelity is much more prevalent today.

Unfortunately, there is not enough data to determine whether or not such sins are on the rise. Even the confidential survey (three hundred pastors) conducted by Christianity Today, Inc. for *Leadership*, a magazine read mostly by ministers, is only partially helpful without other corroborating data. The guilty may be less likely to admit the truth than the innocent, thus skewing the data.

However, *Leadership's* survey suggests that we do have a serious problem in the church. Approximately 33 percent of the pastors surveyed had confessed to "sexually inappropriate" behavior with someone other than their spouse. Another 18 percent admitted to "other forms of sexual contact with someone other than their spouse, i.e., passionate kissing, fondling, mutual masturbation," while in the ministry. Of the ministers polled, 12 percent acknowledged having had sexual intercourse with someone other than their spouse since they've been in local church ministry. When asked about the person with whom they had "sexual intercourse or other forms of sexual contact," 52 percent of the adulterous pastors said it was someone on their church staff or in their congregation; another 17 percent said the other person was a counselee.[2] Of the pastors who admitted to illicit sexual contact, only 4 percent indicated that their congregations had uncovered their infidelity.[3]

THE GOOD NEWS

Forgive me for being an optimist on this subject, but I would like to point out that on the basis of this survey, 88 percent of the pastors in this country have never committed adultery. Also 82 percent have done nothing sexually explicit, including passionate kissing. And 77 percent have never done anything that was "sexually inappropriate" in any way. In this sexually charged day, over three-fourths of today's ministers have *never* behaved in a sexually inappropriate way. We need to hear more about that crowd![4]

These statistics should give great comfort to church members everywhere. Obviously, the overwhelming majority of ministers can be trusted, even in this age of sexual license.

However, some congregations and families take no comfort from these numbers. Their minister—their husband or father—*was* involved in adultery. And they continue to feel the unbearable pain and shame that accompanies the exposure of sexual sin. It is to these congregations and families that I dedicate this book.

THE BIG QUESTIONS THIS BOOK WILL ANSWER

When we hear of a pastor's infidelity, our first question is often *why?* Why would a dedicated minister of the gospel jeopardize his entire career and subject those he loves to such torture and despair? I don't pretend to have all the answers, but I can offer some I have discovered through the years. Part I explores factors that contribute to a minister's fall and ways that ministers can avoid sexual temptation.

But a more significant question remains: Can a minister who has fallen sexually be restored to ministry? Frankly, the Bible is not clear on that subject, and Christian leaders articulate a variety of opinions. Unfortunately, some of our largest denominations have no set pattern for dealing with the problem. Part II describes how a church can deal with ministerial infidelity and explores several positions about restoring fallen ministers. I pray that this book can provide some fresh ideas that will have a positive impact on a church that has been rocked by ministerial infidelity.

CHAPTER 2

The High Cost of Ministerial Infidelity

Can a man scoop fire into his lap without his clothes being burned? Can a man walk on hot coals without his feet being scorched? So is he who sleeps with another man's wife; no one who touches her will go unpunished. But a man who commits adultery lacks judgment; whoever does so destroys himself. For the prostitute reduces you to a loaf of bread, and the adulteress preys upon your very life.

King Solomon (Prov. 6:27–29, 32, 26)

*U*ntil you have put your arms around a minister friend who has been exposed for the sin of adultery—both hearing and feeling the soul-wrenching sobs that wrack him to the depths of his being at the loss of his ministry, integrity, self-respect, and perhaps even his marriage—you have never really heard a man express grief.

I am not unaccustomed to human distress. As a pastor for thirty-five years, I have seen parents lose children, couples bury partners, and individuals endure almost every conceivable type of suffering. Many times I could only hold them in my arms and cry with them. Words at such a time are often meaningless. One must simply "weep with those that weep."

Yet in my experience, the greatest expression of pain has been voiced by a fellow minister who is crushed by the shame his adultery has brought to his Lord, the church, and everyone he loves. Some men have sobbed long after their eyes can no longer produce tears. The fallen minister can find no light at the end of his tunnel. He faces an endless darkness—and has no one to blame but himself.

THE HIGH COST TO THE MINISTER

Adultery is never a private sin. And ministerial adultery has far-reaching effects, including not only the minister, his ministry, his wife, and his family, but also the other woman and her family, the church, Christianity, and non-Christians.

Adultery is a sin that the church of Jesus Christ doesn't take lightly. Scripture so frequently castigates the sin of becoming "one flesh" with anyone other than one's own wife or husband that it labels it a sin against the person's own body (1 Cor. 6:18). Other passages identify it as a sin against the soul, meaning literally, "your life" (Prov. 6:32).

While recently having dinner with a sixty-seven-year-old pastor of a Midwestern church, I told him about the adultery of a close pastor friend and asked, "Have you ever known God to restore a man to a ministry comparable in effectiveness to the one he had before his sexual fall?" The man looked at me in silence. In fact, the silence lasted so long that I became uncomfortable. Then tears began to stream down his face. When he finally found his voice, he replied, "Brother LaHaye, I haven't mentioned this for nine years, but when I was a young man, I had an affair with a woman in the congregation." He then reviewed the tragic results. And it was obvious that time, God's forgiveness, and even divine blessing on his current ministry hadn't removed the sorrow, shame, and grief of his sin—not even after thirty-three years.

Frankly, I don't believe a sincere minister who falls into this sin can feel anything but devastating torment. For that reason I caution Christians not to heap undue suffering on fallen ministers; they usually heap enough on themselves. As one might expect, a spirit of rage usually wells up in the hearts of parishioners when they first learn of their pastor's sin. "He should pay!" they snarl, exuding a smug self-righteousness. Believe me, he has! We don't lessen the gravity of his sin or soften the consequences of his actions when we remind ourselves that nothing we can do to him will exceed the weight of his own self-guilt.

Unfortunately, long after a pastor's public humiliation, some Christians are obsessed with the notion that he should receive a double penalty for his sins. If only they could see him up close during his hours of sorrow, weighted down with a grief that reduces a formerly effective spiritual leader to continual tears—not for hours but for days. Several such men have been suicidal during those long nights when they couldn't sleep. Most painful to them is knowing that they have betrayed their Lord.

One minister friend, whose ministry I have admired for many years, was exposed publicly as an adulterer. My human reaction to the media reports was typical: I was furious with him. As I flew across the country to see him, I couldn't help asking, "Why would he jeopardize such a fabulous ministry that God has used to help thousands of people?" I thought to myself, *I could kill him!* I was unaware that I could even think such thoughts. And I thought I meant it—until I saw him. When I looked into that formerly handsome face, now etched with lines of grief and despair, I could only wrap my arms around him and cry with him. Yes, I still loved him. And I still asked why. But the anger had vanished. It couldn't withstand the pathetic sight of his agony.

All angry, vindictive Christians should have been present after one of my friends, a highly respected man of God, had written out his resignation. He read it through one last time before handing it to the chairman of his deacon board. Then he put his face in his hands and wept so profusely that his tears trickled through his fingers. "My God, my God, what have I done? What have I done? What have I done?" he sobbed. There wasn't an angry heart in the room—nor a dry eye.

His Ministry Will Never Be the Same

A minister is subjected to excruciating pain when he falls into the sin of adultery. He suddenly recognizes that his ministry is gone. His life will never be the same.

Every morning when he looks in the mirror, he will see an adulterer—a forgiven adulterer (if he has truly repented of his sin), but one who, like David, will cry, "My sin is always before me" (Ps. 51:3b). And that may be the highest cost of all: his inability to forgive himself. King David lived like a man after God's own heart most of his life, and in his case adultery, deceit, and murder occupied only a short period of his eighty years on earth. But even David bore the consciousness of that short-term sin to his grave.

One close minister friend, who had developed a strong missionary program in his church, fell in love with a missionary wife who was home on furlough and participating in a missions conference at the minister's church. Who would have dreamed that before her furlough was over, my minister friend would leave his wife and his church, to move in with that missionary wife?

In the beginning he rejected words of remonstrance from me and other minister friends. But when God finally reached him, he broke off his illicit relationship. I then had the privilege of counseling him and his wife as they made a reconciliation. Some time later he took a church in another part of the country and was seemingly blessed of the Spirit of God.

After about five years, my friend contracted brain cancer

and died a long, horribly painful death. Incidentally, I don't look on his cancer as the result of sin, because he repented of that sin, and the Bible clearly teaches, "If we judge ourselves, we would not come under judgment" (1 Cor. 11:31). And while I believe God could send disease to unrepentant Christians whose evil ways are a reproach to the cause of Christ, I don't believe he delivers such judgment on those who confess their sin. In fact, the Bible affirms that the Lord forgives our "wickedness and will remember [our] sins no more" (Jer. 31:34b).

Unfortunately, my fallen minister friend could not fully relinquish his sense of guilt. Several times during the last weeks of his life, he would cry, "This never would have happened if I had not sinned." He would add in anguish, "Tim, the worst part is, I don't believe God has forgiven me!" My friend knew better than that, for he had helped thousands of people with the assurance of divine forgiveness. But when he needed it most, he failed to gain that assurance for himself. His sin became a barrier to a full acceptance of God's mercy.

A minister who has had a sexual affair not only faces guilt and loss of self-respect, but he also loses the respect of his congregation. He is never quite sure that his friends aren't viewing him with contempt. And if he resigns his church, cultural shock sets in: he no longer receives the respect that is unique to ministers. All the credit and esteem he enjoyed as an active pastor has vanished.

Once he loses his ministerial base, even for honorable reasons, he soon learns that he has lost not only his job but also his integrity. No matter how effective his ministry had been before his fall, he often is remembered for his sin, not his good deeds—at least for the first few months, and probably for two to five years.

Christians are very intolerant of ministers who divorce to marry another woman and still attempt to retain their ministry. Women are particularly intolerant because it sends a negative message to their husbands: "If it doesn't work out, get a divorce." With the national divorce rate running at 50 percent, we don't need that message in the church. Besides, I have found few situations where a married couple couldn't reconcile and learn to love each other all over again if they really sought God's will.

One of my minister friends was told by a Christian author who had divorced his wife, "Don't worry about it. Divorce your wife and marry the woman you're in love with. In three years the Christian community will forget all about it, and your books will be as popular as ever." But he was wrong! The Christian community hasn't and won't forget about it. Neither of these men has the public or private ministry he once enjoyed or could have had. I happen to know that my friend's wife would have taken him back and worked diligently to preserve their marriage, but he refused to give up seeing the other woman. Today he has a difficult time understanding why many Christians and most reputable publishers are unwilling to treat him as if nothing happened.

His Marriage Will Never Be the Same

Marriage is a sacred relationship between two members of the opposite sex and God. Most of all, it is a contract of sexual exclusivity "for as long as you both shall live." And while a minister may admit at first that he has sinned against God, he soon realizes that he has also sinned deeply against his wife. He must face her with the truth that although he had vowed to be faithful to her, he has broken that contract. In many cases, the husband will lament, "This will kill my wife!" or "She will never forgive me!"

According to the New Testament, the minister's wife now has the scriptural right to divorce him if she so chooses (Matt. 19:9). Adultery is a damaging sin. Not only has the pastor sinned against his own body, but he also has sinned against his wife's body (see 1 Cor. 6:18; 7:4). Many women have said to their husbands, "If there's one thing I could never forgive, it's adultery."

Despite the pain that the minister's wife will feel, if she is a godly woman, she will forgive her husband if he is repentant. I haven't seen any poll data, but I have found that about 85 percent of the pastor's wives I have counseled have found the grace to forgive their adulterous husbands—but it is *never* easy.

However, forgiving and forgetting are two different matters. One fallen pastor confided in me that for several years when he crawled into bed with his wife, his expressions of love enraged her. Instead of responding affectionately, she would cry, express anger, and beat on his chest, flailing him for his sin. Only by summoning the grace of a forgiving God could he take her wrists in his hand, forcibly preventing her from beating him, and urge, "Sweetheart, you have every right to feel this way. I sinned against God and against you. I am terribly sorry. Please forgive me."

The wife isn't the only person who finds it hard to forget. From the time of his infidelity, the fallen pastor will never again possess the free-of-guilt spirit of the faithful husband when he approaches his wife for love. Instead, every closing of his bedroom door will be a reminder of betrayal, not faithfulness. In most cases, he will spend the rest of his life trying to prove his love.

One of the greatest losses a marriage will sustain is the loss of love and respect. In his teaching to husbands and wives, the apostle Paul says: "However, each one of you also must *love* his wife as he loves himself, and the wife must *respect* her husband" (Eph. 5:33, emphasis added). Paul suggests that a husband's love and a wife's respect are two essential ingredients in a godly marriage—and both of these elements are lost in the husband's infidelity. The one thing a husband values over any other gift his wife can give him is her respect.

A minister's wife may never regain respect for her

husband after his fall. If she indulges in anger and doesn't truly forgive him, merely going through the motions of taking him back, their relationship will be miserable.

In fairness to most of the godly Christian wives I have tried to help through this process, if a woman's commitment to the ministry matches that of her husband when he accepted the call, her love will be demonstrated by trying to inflict a minimum of pain on her fallen partner. More than anyone else, she sees and feels the depth of his pain. She shares the letters he receives from people he has helped through this or similar sins, and she watches helplessly as he is crushed by their critical wrath. But even though godly wives are more apt to respect their husbands in spite of their sin, it is never easy. That is all part of the high cost of sin.

His Family Will Never Be the Same

If the loss of his wife's respect isn't enough, facing his crushed and disconsolate children is a formidable task. They usually cry with their father at first, responding in forgiveness. But when the extent of his sin becomes apparent through the graphic changes in their personal lives, they often turn on him in anger and delight in inflicting the pain of disrespect—if not in words, then in their actions or looks of contempt. In many cases, however, the unreasonable persecution he is subjected to by the disappointed, angry members of the congregation cause the children to rally to their father with support. However, relations are rarely the same between them—at least for many years.

And the cost to the minister for this sin goes on and on, seemingly well out of proportion to his deed. Or is it? He has sinned not just against his Lord and the woman involved, but against his wife and family, against the family of his sexual partner, against his church, his denomination, his community, and the cause of Christ. It is almost impossible to exaggerate the far-reaching consequences of a minister's infidelity.

THE HIGH COST TO THE MINISTER'S WIFE

In talking with the wives of fallen ministers, I have been amazed that they are rarely surprised. Although they have buried certain suspicions in their hearts for "lack of firm evidence," as one said, their intuition finally proved to be accurate. Even so, they are never ready for the ugly truth.

To the godly wife whose pastor husband must tell her he has had sexual relations with another woman, it is a devastating experience. Her dreams are dashed, and cold, naked fear grips her heart.

Her Life Will Never Be the Same

Whether or not the wife realizes it at the time of her husband's confession, the consequences of his action have changed her life. The effects of his adulterous relationship will take her emotions on an unprecedented roller-coaster ride for months and possibly years to come. Her first response may be tears. She may be moved by her husband's grief, weeping with him and offering her forgiveness.

But hard on the heels of grief may be the wife's most significant response—anger. She may confront for the first time in her life the cauldron of natural anger that boils and rages within. Her anger may swing from peaks of fury to more moderate periods of resentment. She may have been an experienced practitioner of the Spirit-controlled life and one who has learned to give thanks in every situation, but it may take some time before she responds spiritually to this sin.

Her resentment will often diminish, if not eliminate, her sexual desire for her husband. Anger does that. I have been convinced for years that anger is a more powerful emotion than love. Unless she truly seeks God's grace for forgiveness and help in "forgetting," her resentment can make her a very cold woman. Several betrayed women have acknowledged to me that within three months of their husbands' admission of guilt, "I have no feeling for my husband. Making love is no longer a pleasure; it is a gruesome duty." Such an admission proves that they are deeply angry.

A wife's emotions are further tested in her relationships to her children and family. She is usually the one who must comfort children who are confused and possibly angered by their father's actions. She is usually the one who must face the relatives.

And the wife's emotions are not the only part of her that is affected by her husband's infidelity. If the infidelity is made public to the church, the family will need to resign, necessitating a move. In addition, their salary usually takes an enormous drop, though some churches thoughtfully continue a fallen pastor's salary for three to twelve months. Sooner or later, however, her husband will have to find another job. She also may have to seek employment outside the home for the first time.

Her Ministry Will Never Be the Same

A minister's infidelity often will cause the wife to lose *her* ministry as well. She may have been actively involved in the church, and her husband's sin will seriously fracture her relationships to people in the church. One such wife, teacher of a large women's Bible class, fretted, "His sin has cost me my ministry—and I haven't done anything wrong!"

As one who has been humiliated, the minister's wife must bear some of the results of her husband's moral hypocrisy. People who looked up to her may feel that her life was a charade, at least for a time. She will wonder what the people of the church think about her now. Many will blame her partially for being less than warm and sexually responsive, and some will assume that she was cold and even frigid.

26

While she may not be guilty of any sin or neglect, she will feel the disapproval of her former friends, and seldom will she escape some of the blame for the disruption and shame this sin has brought to the whole congregation.

Even wives who lean on God for his grace and learn to love their husbands all over again may never stop paying the price of that sin. At many of the Family Life Seminars or conferences where Bev and I speak, women identify themselves as former pastors' wives and acknowledge, "I really miss my life and ministry in the pastorate."

The months after the minister's wife learns of her husband's infidelity are filled with grisly reminders of the high cost she must pay for his sin. The words of her wedding vows, "for better or for worse," take on new meaning for her.

The High Cost of Forgiveness

One wife who learned of her husband's infidelity came for counseling. After we talked and prayed together, she forgave her husband.

But she was back in my office in three months. "I can no longer respond to my husband," she confessed. "I can't even stand to have him touch me!"

Humanly speaking, we can understand her wrath. I explained to her, "Your anger and resentment have turned you off sexually."

"What should I do?" she asked.

I pointed her to Philippians 3:13 and encouraged her to "forgive him and forget the things that are behind you."

I wasn't prepared for her angry response. "He doesn't deserve forgiveness! We were both raised in a Bible-teaching church. He knew better than that! I don't think I can ever forgive him."

I knew that she was really admitting that she didn't *want* to forgive him. And if she didn't want to forgive him, I knew she wouldn't. I finally asked her, "Do you want to be happy or miserable the rest of your life?"

She responded in tears, "I want to be happy, of course!"

"Then you will have to forgive him," I insisted. "Not because he deserves it, but because it is God's will for you."

And with God's help she did forgive him. Today they have a beautiful relationship and a solid marriage. Not only is his sin forgiven, but their relationship is healed, and they are together again serving the Lord. But it wasn't easy for her. It never is.

THE HIGH COST TO THE FAMILY

While flying to a western city, a colleague of mine sat next to an attractive college sophomore. My friend could tell she wasn't far from tears. The Spirit of God led him to ask, "Is something troubling you?"

She burst into tears and finally revealed the story of a life tragically changed by her minister father's infidelity. "One week ago I was big on campus. My father was a well-known minister and Christian leader in our denomination. Two days ago he resigned our church in disgrace; the word spread through our school, and everything changed. Now I am the daughter of a fallen minister."

For her—and for all fallen ministers' children—that is only the beginning. The word of ministerial infidelity spreads rapidly. The children feel the loss of respect, projected not only from other young people but at times from teachers as well.

One minister's son was heard to scream at his father, his former idol, "I knew you were a hypocrite all the time. I never want to see you again." This kind of anger compounds the heartache for both parents.

Some children use their father's infidelity to excuse their own behavior. One senior in a Christian school sponsored by his father's former church got his girlfriend pregnant. When the young man was confronted, he responded, "Like father, like son." A minister's daughter, who as far as her parents knew was a virgin before her father's public humiliation, became so promiscuous that she seduced three of her classmates, necessitating expulsion for all four young people from the Christian school where they were enrolled.

Some rebellious ministers' kids are known to use their father's sin as an excuse to be angry with God. Although they must know that their parents have devoutly prayed that their children will choose to walk in truth, they rebel against God. One of the current leaders of an anti-Christian organization is the angry son of a fallen minister.

Brokenhearted Christian parents related this tragic story to me. Their deeply spiritual son felt called to become a preacher and as a high-school senior had been looking forward to attending a Christian college. His girlfriend was the popular and virtuous daughter of the dynamic pastor under whose ministry the son had grown up. Unfortunately, this pastor committed adultery. When his daughter learned of her father's sin, her behavior changed. She became sexually aggressive and one night seduced the young man. Within a few weeks she learned she was pregnant! The lives of these two young people were radically changed. In her youthful anger to spite her father, this young girl ruined two lives and brought heartache to many. Perhaps that is what Moses meant when he said that God "does not leave the guilty unpunished; he punishes the children and their children for the sin of the fathers to the third and fourth generation" (Ex. 34:7).

But it isn't just the children who suffer. In most cases the infidelity produces enough hurt to flood the extended family, particularly the minister's parents and parents-in-law. Most ministers' parents are very proud of the fact that their son is a pastor. This pleasure is dashed to pieces when they learn of their son's fall into disgrace.

The extent of the pain caused by this one sin is

incredible. I can't think of a single family member that is not affected. One mother I know carried her hurt to an early grave. She concluded her life saying, "God forgive my son _____."

THE HIGH COST TO THE CHURCH

One sign of God's grace in the church is that it has weathered not only the storms of dictators, kings, and antagonists, but also the sins of its leaders. Here we are, closing in on the twenty-first century, and the church is alive and well, growing worldwide.

However, next to a church split, the most devastating event in a church's existence is a pastor's fall into public humiliation due to adultery. Ministerial adultery disillusions the church, the young people, the regular tithers, and the lost. In addition, it affects the witness and reputation of the church to the community, particularly to the unsaved.

Enormous frustration usually follows a pastor's confession of adultery, especially if the adultery involved another person from the church. Most often the pastor resigns, either voluntarily or at the decision of the church board. Families and lifetime friends often can be divided in their loyalties, and many weak Christians can be caused to stumble by the example of their former shepherd. One church known for its peace and harmony erupted in such bitterness that opposing sides threatened violence against each other.

Churches do rise above such trials, through much prayer and love. But even at best ministerial adultery leaves scars that last for years. Chapter 6 discusses ways a church can weather this storm with a minimum of damage to its long-range ministry.

THE HIGH COST TO CHRISTIANITY

For as long as I can remember, ministers, priests, and rabbis were among the most admired of all men—until the recent televangelist scandals. While the Christian church will survive, there is no question it has been damaged by the blasphemy the evangelists' sins have precipitated. Unbelievers have always enjoyed ridiculing the church, but the recent scandals have been new grist for the mills of anti-Christian journalists, reporters, and college professors.

Some of the ridicule, from late-night comedians to derisive program character assassinations, has done little to let the scandals die. In addition, each time a government investigation is begun, it is given prominent coverage in our nation's media. Many Christians seem to live each day with the dreaded question, "Who will be next?"

The good news is that many people recognize that the church is led by human members of Adam's race and hold *individuals* accountable for their misdeeds, not the whole body of Christ. But no one denies that the reputation of the Christian church is damaged when its leaders fall.

Another cost to the church for pastoral immorality is financial loss. As the result of the loss of confidence in televangelists, fund raising for some television and radio ministries has fallen off more than 35 percent. Some ministries have been canceled, and others have been seriously cut back. Jerry Falwell alone had to take his one-hour gospel program off over fifty stations, and Robert Schuller acknowledges the most severe financial crisis in his entire ministry—as do Dr. D. James Kennedy and others. And none of these men were involved in even the slightest moral scandal.

THE HIGH COST TO THE LOST

While flying in a plane bound for Washington, D.C., a minister began talking with the man next to him, an employee of the federal government. The minister began to talk about his faith when the federal employee smirked. "I suppose you're one of these TV evangelists I've been reading about," he said.

"No," the minister responded. "I do some TV and radio work, but my moral life is above reproach. I sincerely try to live what I preach."

The government man, who classified himself as an agnostic, asked, "How do I know you aren't just like the rest of them?" And he wouldn't listen to another word the minister uttered.

That may not be a representative case, but for those who seek an excuse to reject our Lord, the sexual misconduct of ministers provides one ready-made. While the excuse won't survive Judgment Day, it may be enough to convince a person to reject God's offer of grace. Recently I counseled a man who indicated that his protracted rebellion against God could be traced to the career-destroying moral sin of a minister he had admired as a young man. The moral sin of this minister had caused the young man to stumble. We must admit that only eternity will reveal the harm done to unbelievers when a minister falls.

WHO CAN MEASURE LOST POTENTIAL?

The minister of a growing church shared with me his deepest dreams about his future ministry. It was incredible! If God would have fulfilled his dreams, this man would have pastored the largest church in the country.

But today all those dreams are mere dreams! The minister's sexual sin has transformed his dreams into nightmares.

If this minister hadn't fallen, many more people could have been reached for Christ. This tarnished vessel will never accomplish in his lifetime what was possible if he had been faithful both to God and to his wife.

That will always be the case! We need to remember the apostle Paul's words, "Everyone who competes in the games goes into strict training. They do it to get a crown that will not last; but we do it to get a crown that will last forever.

Therefore I do not run like a man running aimlessly; I do not fight like a man beating the air. No, I beat my body and make it my slave so that after I have preached to others, I myself will not be disqualified for the prize" (1 Cor. 9:25–27).

Hardly a week goes by but I hear of another minister or Christian leader whose moral conduct has disqualified him from the ministry. He apparently forgot the sobering maxim:

> *You can spend your life*
> *any way you like.*
> *But you can only spend it*
> *once!*

CHAPTER 3

Why Ministers Fall into Sexual Sin

Most of the ministers who have been involved in sexual sin never thought it would happen to them. They were dedicated, godly men whom God used mightily in the lives of others. In some cases, their very effectiveness made them vulnerable to temptation.

The majority of the fallen ministers I have counseled were sincere pastors who faithfully preached God's Word, led many people to Christ, and were literally consumed by the work of God—until they became involved in sexual sin and the bottom fell out of their lives.

When a minister is involved in sexual sin, people ask the obvious question: Why? Why did he do it? We assume he didn't intend to. We muse, "It just happened." But that is not true. It never "just happens"!

Sexual sin is always the result of progressive steps, any one of which should have warned the pastor long before he jumped into bed with the wrong woman. At crucial points of vulnerability in his life, he made a small compromise, then another, until the sin was unavoidable. The ultimate fall resulted from choice, not chance.

Remember David? He stayed home when he should have gone to war. Then he watched a beautiful woman bathing on a nearby rooftop. Instead of turning away, he continued to stare, and eventually his look turned to lust. Finally he sent for her—and the rest is tragic history.

The majority of ministers—the 88 percent that the *Leadership* survey indicates have *not* committed adultery— have been tempted, and at some point many of them may have compromised mentally. But they caught themselves before that compromise led to a bigger one and finally to overt sexual sin.

What are those progressive steps, those compromises that can lead a minister to be involved in sexual sin? I believe we can identify several forces, attitudes, and values that can corrode a minister's moral life and make him vulnerable to a sexual affair.

FORCES THAT CAN LEAD TO SEXUAL SIN

Many fallen ministers have said that they had underestimated their own vulnerability. They had not seriously considered the power of certain forces over their life, and as a result, they had not safeguarded themselves against these powers.

The Power of Sexual Attraction

A minister spends much of his time with the women of his congregation: married women, single women, fulfilled and godly women. Many ministers are naïve about the power of sexual attraction these women may have on him.

I have maintained an unscientific theory for many years: all people have an emotional-physical magnetic attraction to other people. I mentioned it twenty years ago in my book *How to Be Happy Though Married,* and today I am more than ever convinced of it.

For reasons we can only guess, certain people are more attractive to us than others—and not primarily because of appearance. We can sometimes feel that magnetic attraction to a rather plain person of the opposite sex yet feel none at all to a beautiful or handsome person. I once had a very beautiful secretary. Several visiting pastors kidded me about her, but she never once revved my motor. I enjoyed working with her, but sexually we were not on the same wavelength. That isn't true of all women. In the presence of some women, I feel an unseen magnetic attraction and have to work hard at avoiding these situations.

Ministers are in a vulnerable position. From the pulpit and the counseling office, they project a gracious, understanding, wise, and gentle image—just what every woman yearns for in a man. It is only natural that grateful women are attracted to their ministers and appreciate his kindness to them. But if they aren't careful, adoration may lead to adultery.

One subtle aspect of this was conveyed to me by Dr. Donald Grey Barnhouse when I was a very young pastor. "It is always the minister's responsibility to safeguard his moral relationship to women." He then pointed out that women intuitively know they are the "moral policemen" in all their relationships with men. They are the ones that limit a man's expressions of intimate affection—except with a minister. Their respect for him as a man of God is such that they tend to lower the moral safeguard in respect for what they imagine to be his superior spiritual life, entrusting their conduct to him. They forget that the man of God is first and foremost a *man*. In this sexually charged day, contacts between the sexes are most easily regulated when both parties guard the relationship.

One of the wise pastors who recognizes this problem, yet maintains a heavy counseling load, makes a point of limiting his counseling of any woman. After three sessions he refers her to someone else. He also restricts any discussion of a sexually intimate nature to one session. For any further interviews, he insists that another member of his staff sit in to observe.

The Power of Seductive Women

Some of the women a minister counsels or works with do not have pure motives in their relationship to him. I would venture to say that 2–4 percent of the women in a congregation are unfulfilled in their marriage or are in some way emotionally and sexually starved. They begin fantasizing about their pastor, and before long their lust becomes aggressive. And unless a pastor recognizes her conscious or unconscious intentions, he becomes vulnerable.

I once had an encounter with a woman who later brought down a minister friend. She was absolutely gorgeous, labeled by some a Farrah Fawcett look-alike. She was also a toucher. Several times after my Bible class she came up to comment on the study—and was overpowering. Even my tired old heart skipped a beat! It was good that I have never been attracted to aggressive women, and I recognized immediately that she was a male headhunter. Even my wife noticed it. When the woman invited us over for dinner, we thanked her and said we would call some Saturday night when we were both scheduled to be in town. We had walked no further than fifteen feet from the woman when I heard my wife say, "We will *not* be going to their house!"

Unfortunately, my minister friend didn't identify the woman as an emotional stick of dynamite—and today he is out of the ministry. Frankly, I carry a degree of guilt for not being smart enough to have warned him. I protected myself, but I didn't think of defending him. Since then, at the risk of alienating my minister friends, I confront them from time to time in a friendly attempt to hold them morally accountable.

I have no difficulty believing the many fallen ministers who feel, "If the woman hadn't approached me first, I don't think I would ever have had the affair." This certainly doesn't excuse the minister, but it does point out the power of seductive women. While most church women are not sexually aggressive to anyone but their husband, all ministers should learn to watch out for that small percentage of seductive women. One professional study of first contacts among singles indicated that women made the first contact five times more frequently than men.

The Power of Emotional Bonding

For many fallen ministers the drive to have an affair was not sexual but emotional. Unaware of the emotional bonding that grows between two people in a working/counseling relationship, these pastors began to desire a deeper relationship with certain women. Sometimes their emotional bonding to another woman was the result of weak bonding to their own wives, but even in healthy marriages a minister can compromise and bond to another woman. And once he stumbles into emotional union with another woman, the sexual liaison often follows.

> Peter Kreitler writes in *Affair Prevention:* "Affairs begin not just for sexual reasons but to satisfy the basic need we all have for closeness, goodness, kindness, togetherness—what I call the 'ness' needs. When these needs are not met on a regular basis in a marriage, the motivation may be to find a person who will be good to us, touch us, hold us, give us a feeling of closeness. Sexual fulfillment may indeed become an important part of an extramarital relationship, but the 'ness' needs are, for most men and women I know, initially more important."[1]

Several of the men I know who destroyed their ministries had an adulterous affair with women who were physically less attractive than their own wives. In each case, adultery was occasioned by a weak emotional bonding to their wife, making them vulnerable when they met a woman with whom they developed a strong emotional bond.

If counseling pastors would admit it, they probably spend more time paying attention to some of their counselees than they do their own wives. In fact, many pastors develop a bond with several women, failing to realize how potentially dangerous it is.

In his excellent book *Perils of Power: Immorality in the Ministry,* Richard Exley said, "Emotional bonding is often the first step toward infidelity, and nothing facilitates such bonding faster than an emotionally deprived woman and a compassionate pastor whose marriage and personal life are unfulfilling."[2]

Frequently this lack of emotional bonding with his wife is the pastor's own fault. His attitude and conduct at home may have killed his wife's respect for him, which makes it difficult for her to "stroke" him when he needs it. And let's face it, unless he walks in the Spirit all the time, even a minister needs stroking. But it is difficult for even the most devoted wife to maintain respect for a husband who doesn't live at home what he preaches at church. She sees women fawn over him at church, looking at him as if he were a saint, the answer to every woman's dream. When women in the church tell her, "It must be wonderful to be married to such an ideal Christian," she is tempted to ask, "Which minister? The one at church or the one I see at home?" This resentment can rob them of "togetherness" even when they are together, which often destroys what emotional bonding they do possess. At such a time, the pastor is vulnerable to a woman who shares his interests, values—and emotional need.

One friend destroyed his marriage and ministry by developing a bond with the church secretary. These were not morally depraved people, just two vulnerable people who never should have worked so closely together. Adultery wasn't on the horizon when they discovered they could talk to each other about anything. She was married to a man who gave her little love and almost no companionship. His marriage was antagonistic from the beginning; nothing he did ever pleased his wife. Eventually, then, two terribly unhappy people, traveling a rather barren desert, found oasis in each other. It wasn't passion; it wasn't lust. Their affair was the natural result of an unnatural emotional bonding that should be reserved for only one person on earth: one's lifetime companion. I have found few ministers who have built a strong, emotional bond with their spouse and succumbed to adultery—no matter how tempting it was.

But you may ask, "What should a minister who is not emotionally bonded to his wife do when he finds someone with whom he does feel such a bond?" The answer is easier to give than to live, but it is biblical: "*Flee* youthful lusts" (2 Tim. 2:22 NKJV, emphasis added). If my minister friend had dismissed that secretary and avoided any one-to-one contact with her, he would have saved both of their families—not to mention the cause of Christ—much damage.

ATTITUDES THAT CAN LEAD TO A MORAL FALL

Pride

After many years of observing ministers who have become involved in sexual affairs, I am convinced that what opens his heart to the temptation to commit adultery is *pride*. The minister's pride may be a lifetime pattern or a temporary phase that results from the power of the pulpit.

When God powerfully uses a minister and he sees peoples' lives changed, he often is tempted to take credit for what God has done. When people tell him he is a great preacher and that his sermons have changed their lives, he is tempted to pat himself on the back—and that is dangerous, deadly dangerous!

A minister is human. He likes stroking, too—particularly

to offset the criticism and harsh judgment he may hear from some church members. So when people tell him what a good job he is doing, his ego may begin to swell. Somehow ministers have to remind themselves all week long how totally dependent they are on God's power for anything eternal to result from their lives. They seem to understand that fact on Saturday night: somehow they need to retain that principle seven days a week.

The minister son of a fallen, fundamentalist preacher asked his father to explain how he got involved in sexual sin. The father's response was honest: "I guess I thought I was so special to God that he wouldn't let anything happen to me."

Pride subtly implies that we are above the law. It is akin to driving a powerful car on a lonely highway. The speed limit is fifty-five miles per hour, but we travel at sixty-five or seventy. Whether or not we know it, we are saying, "I am something special; I am above the law." But when we get caught, we must still pay the fine. The minister who forgets that only the power of God can move audiences and bring sinners to repentance may momentarily reflect, "I am someone special to God; I am above the law." As a result of his false view of reality, he may live without safeguards and wander into situations that he can't handle.

Pride fogs our vision and corrupts our reason. Ministers need to remember that God doesn't overlook moral compromises just because they preach theologically uncompromising sermons. Instead, they need to remember that the same God who requires theological purity also demands moral purity. God requires him to "be holy, because I am holy" (Lev. 11:45b). There are no exceptions!

Another manifestation of pride is a minister's ego. Attention from women—a female staff person, a female counselee, a member of a class the minister may lead, a female outside the church—can be ego building. And if that attention is encouraged and left unchecked, it can eventually lead to adultery.

Using his sacred position to bolster his flagging ego by taking advantage of a woman whose emotional insecurity or spiritual immaturity makes her vulnerable to a man she trusts, a minister of God displays a kind of carnality that has been going on for centuries. A probing question from a woman in one of my former churches revealed a great deal about several ministers in our town. Because the woman was extremely capable, she became secretary of almost every inter-church committee in the city, which threw her into contact with many ministers over the years. With tears she confided in me that so many ministers had made sexual overtures to her that she was losing confidence in all ministers. With intense emotion she added, "Before God, I do not believe I have ever given them any indication that I was a loose woman, but several have treated me as if I were."

I was pleased to assure her that such men were in the minority and that most ministers were her spiritual brothers. The minority, however, were emotionally frustrated men who didn't need a liaison with a woman. They needed to get back on their knees and work out new priorities for their life and ministry and spend more time building a meaningful love relationship with their wife (Eph. 5:25).

Resistance to Accountability

A second attitude that can lead pastors into moral collapse is resistance to accountability. Strong leaders are usually independent people who by nature resist accountability. And the more powerful a person becomes, the more he may reject other peoples' involvement in his life. Even men who start out sincerely seeking to serve God can succumb to the narcotic of power. That's why they need friends, other pastors, family members, or board members who love them enough to hold them accountable.

In my opinion, the most pathetic figure in Jim Bakker's fall was the minister who shared the camera with him on the

PTL show and who shared the pastorate of the church at Heritage Village. How different that whole story would have been if this older minister had treated Jim the same way the apostle Paul treated the apostle Peter and had "opposed him to his face, because he was clearly in the wrong" (Gal. 2:11). Jim needed rebuke when he first showed signs of yielding to the corrupting influence of power. The older pastor may well have been fired had he done so, but at least he would have retained his honor and integrity today, and perhaps Jim Bakker may have heeded his advice.

But it isn't just the famous who have a problem with the corrupting influence of power. Even pastors of small churches can intimidate their boards and associates out of holding them accountable—much to their own peril.

Most pastors are held financially accountable by their church board, but unfortunately, it's easier for a church board to demand financial responsibility than to demand moral accountability—until it is too late. This essentially must be a voluntary involvement by the pastor himself, who is wise enough to realize that the flesh can't be trusted—not even his own.

Bill Hybels, pastor of what may be the fastest-growing church in the country—Willow Creek Community Church in South Barrington, Illinois—talked honestly with his congregation about accountability. After noting that a staff member held him accountable in a minor issue such as parking in a no-parking zone at the church, Pastor Hybels said:

> These have been difficult days for me. I've made a special plea to the elders of our church, to the staff, and to the board of directors to turn up the "watch care" on my life. I'm a sinner. I'm tempted every day. I'm carrying a heavy load. And I want to finish well. But you people will fail me if you don't join in providing "watch care" for my life, and other leaders' lives in this place. If you hear any of us say things that cause you concern, if we do things that cause you concern and you don't bring them to our attention in love, if you don't speak up, then you

are paving the way for the kinds of abuses and scandals that have embarrassed the whole kingdom of God worldwide. Oh, we'd all like to put our heads in the sand and say, "It could never happen here." You make *sure* it never happens here. Read the financial statements that we keep trying to pass out to people in this church. Not enough of you take them. Question things that you don't understand. Call us on matters—in love.

Last week I stood before you and called you on what might have been some carelessness about your not coming to the Communion table. I'm going to call you when I think you're out of line. You may not like that; I'm sorry. You'd better be willing to call me when you think I'm out of line. I may not like that, but that's okay. We're to be each other's keepers. We're all sinners. We're all being tempted. We're all carrying loads. We're all going to fall unless we keep each other on the right track.[3]

In addition to being held accountable by church boards and staffs, a minister should be held accountable by his wife. Resistance to accountability is almost synonymous with future defeat. For that reason I always *require* a fallen minister to tell his wife. He will usually protest, "She will kill me," or "She won't be able to handle it," or "She will divorce me." She may be tempted for a while to fulfill all of those threats, but she rarely does. It is, however, imperative that she be confronted with the facts early so that she can help him on his path to wholeness.

But even before that, a pastor's wife should occasionally look deeply into his eyes and ask, "Honey, have you ever been unfaithful to me?" or "Have you ever been tempted to be unfaithful to me?" In talking to wives of fallen ministers, I have found that few are really surprised when news of the husband's sin becomes public. They will often state, "I think I know who it was and when it occurred." The marriage act is such a uniquely intimate experience that many women know the faithfulness not only of their husband's body but also of his heart.

When asked why she didn't confront her husband

sooner, one wife commented, "I didn't have proof; it was just something I felt deep inside. But since I saw God using my husband in a marvelous way, I thought it was just my imagination." I would advise every wife who is suspicious of her husband's morals to watch, pray, and lovingly confront. Unless he is a skilled deceiver, he will betray himself to this woman who shares his life and to whom he has pledged his faithfulness. If he has done no wrong, he will rarely get angry. If he has entered the temptation stage, this confrontation can open the door for him to admit his guilt, which can save both people much heartache. If he flares, he probably has something to hide.

If a wife is suspicious of her husband, she should risk his anger and find out if he is involved with another woman. This is no time for her to crawl into her shell of self-protection, for her very world is in jeopardy. However, a wife must make sure that her suspicions aren't simply the result of her own insecurities. As I have noted, she should watch and pray, then lovingly confront—and name the woman who has aroused her suspicions, even if she has no hard evidence. If her husband is tempted, he may receive her confrontation as a life preserver and welcome her attempt to rescue him.

Anger

The pastor of a large church in our city came in for counseling with his wife. Frankly, I was surprised, for he was my friend; we had worked together on several projects in our city, though we were not of the same denomination. But his wife made it instantly clear how she had coerced him into coming with her: she threatened to divorce him if he refused!

She came right to the point. "Our marriage is in a shambles! I have committed adultery three times with a man in our church; my husband knows all about it, and if he doesn't change, I plan to divorce him!" You may not believe it, but she just was not that kind of woman. This mother of three, married twenty-three years, had deliberately seduced a man in their church just to spite her husband, apparently a model pastor and excellent preacher—even she admitted that. "The trouble with him is that he is two-faced! At church he is kind and gentle, always available to help hurting people. At home he is angry, touchy, and hostile. He disciplines the children too severely for even the slightest things, and he has driven our twenty-one-year-old son away from God, the church, and now even me."

His defense? "I'm a busy pastor with a growing congregation. I work eighteen hours a day. I face lots of frustration in my work. When I come home, I don't want a lot of hassle. It just makes me even more angry."

And that was the problem—he was an angry man. So when he acted like himself at home, he was irritable. In fact, when things didn't please him at church, he would never reveal his hostility. He was so "spiritual" that he waited until dinner time, then vented his pent-up hostilities all over his family—an excellent way to destroy a marriage and children!

I don't mean to belittle my friend, for he was basically a good man—a dedicated, hardworking pastor, called of God to preach. But he was continually frustrated by the growing details, pressures, and expectations of his congregation and himself. Instead of realizing that anger is a sin that grieves the Holy Spirit, he used the people he loved most as his escape valve and turned his wife into a shrew.

Amazingly, she admitted that she still loved him, and he claimed to love her. But his anger had cooled her toward him sexually. Once the pastor was able to see what his behavior had done to his wife and family, he poured out his repentance to God and to her. They were in each other's arms even before they rose from their knees, and the last time I saw them, they reported that their love was stronger than ever.

Many angry ministers are not so blessed. Bringing home frustration, disappointment, and anger from church conflicts, they shatter relationships with those they really love. Once they have alienated their family through their constant anger, they become vulnerable to emotional bonding with other women—women against whom they would never consider venting their anger. If a voluptuous counselee appears in his office or if a sympathetic work associate, sensing his frustration, extends arms of sympathy, he can end up in the wrong bed. He is not a moral degenerate but an angry man who gradually becomes vulnerable to sexual temptation.

VALUES THAT CORRODE A PASTOR'S MORAL LIFE

Modern society places heavy expectations on its leaders, and ministers are no exception. They feel the pressure to be successful, to fulfill all their goals, to work unending hours for the kingdom. Many ministers have found that in placing priority on these values, they have gradually allowed their moral lives to corrode, setting themselves up for a fall.

The Press for Success

Many ministers have bought into the "Alexander-the-Great syndrome," always looking for "more worlds to conquer." But in gaining success, some of them also lost their moral values. This year alone several pastors of super churches and extraordinary ministries have been forced out of ministry for "sexual indiscretions." Johnny Carson reaffirmed the old truism when he commented, "The bigger they are, the harder they fall."

Richard Exley described it well:

> Numerous men have achieved more success than they ever imagined possible only to discover at mid-life, at the height of their career, that they are desperately unfulfilled. This phenomenon is not uncommon in the ministry and often results in a mid-life affair.[4]

Exley further quotes David Seamands, professor of pastoral ministry at Asbury Theological Seminary:

Six college mates in my denomination fell morally at the height of their success. They climbed the Methodist ladder. Two were evangelists, and four were pastors. And the four pastors—in widely separate geographical locations—all had more or less gotten either the top church in the conference or very close to it. They had reached it. That was the moment when down they went. Both evangelists and three of the four pastors are now out of the ministry.

In college, we had noticed these guys had what we called, for want of a better term, "unsurrendered egos." They were gifted people. We could tell they were going to be ladder climbers. They had goals. They lived for them. That kept them clean.

But once you reach your goals, where do you go? What do you do when you've reached the top? They apparently concluded there was nothing else to do, and they went wrong sexually. I've often wondered, however, why all six of these strong and successful ministers fell.

A phrase from C. S. Lewis keeps running through my mind—"the sweet poison of a false infinite." It's a beautiful phrase. They had a false goal: *If I achieve that, I've made it.* That's a false infinite. It's sweet, and it gave them the strength to climb the ladder, but when they got to the top, they did not have the strength to stay there. They fell off. Maybe they self-destructed. But they all did it morally. They got involved with women significantly involved in the church ministry.

What is described here is not unique to the Methodist Church. I've observed the same thing in my own movement, and I'm sure the same thing is occurring in other denominations as well. Highly successful ministers are falling prey to immorality at an alarming rate. Nor is it simply a coincidence that they have succumbed to the tender trap during mid-life, at the height of their careers. By now they have probably achieved more "success" than they ever dreamed possible, and with it more frustration. The minister may be thinking that this

49

is not how he's supposed to feel. Where's the fulfillment, the satisfaction? Who is there to share his achievements? He is probably not intimate with his wife, not even close, and his children are strangers, grown and gone, making a life of their own.

If his public ministry is any indication of his work habits, then it's safe to conclude that he is a confirmed workaholic who thinks nothing of putting in eighty to ninety hours a week. Suddenly, at mid-life, he realizes the futility of it all, but he's at a loss to make a change. He doesn't know anything else. Lonely and depressed, he's especially vulnerable to the temptation of a mid-life affair.[5]

As I read these tragic stories, I was struck by the fact that I didn't recognize any of them—probably because I come from a different denominational background. But I do know several men just like them—and their fall has been devastating. I would add, however, that such men are vulnerable to pride like few I know. All their rave notices have been good ones. If they're not careful, they start believing them, and pride will prove their undoing.

The Drive to Fulfill Goals

All ministers have goals and dreams they wish to accomplish in the ministry. In this day of super churches and televangelists who minister to millions, sometimes ministers set unrealistically high goals. Consequently, even though God uses them in the lives of many, their expectations may never be fully realized.

We are goal-oriented creatures, and goals provide us with the best source of motivation. That is why Paul challenged us to "set [our] hearts on things above" and why our Lord said, "Where your treasure is, there your heart will be also" (Col. 3:1; Matt. 6:21). A minister's heart is filled with church, ministry, Bible teaching, and people helping. If he isn't careful, he may set such a high priority on his ministry goals that he will neglect his family for the church.

Then he may suddenly discover that he isn't going to reach his goals, and he feels as if he has nothing left. The human mind can't tolerate a vacuum, so he is tempted to find another area to provide the fulfillment he so desperately needs. It is at this point that some ministers are vulnerable to extramarital involvements. Unless they are spiritually strong, they may begin to make the little compromises that can lead to sexual sin.

A minister's failure to reach his goals may be even more unsettling if it coincides with a mid-life crisis—that crisis people experience when they first recognize their physical or personal limitations. There is probably no more rewarding work in the world than the pastoral ministry, but therein lies the rub. When he confronts his initial frustration or his first real failure, these accumulated symptoms suddenly grip him, and his crisis begins.

Work, Work, Work

Another value that can corrode a minister's moral life is his perspective about work. Ministers, more than most other professionals, see hard work as a virtue. After all, isn't giving all you've got for the kingdom one of the best ways a man can use his time and energy?

While we are instructed to give ourselves wholeheartedly to the Lord's work, we must be careful not to let our work lead us into two areas of imbalance: workaholism and its close relative, burnout.

Most of the pastors of super churches and the heads of expansive ministries are workaholics. I certainly was—and didn't even try to hide it. In fact, if the truth were known, most workaholic pastors are proud of it.

Perhaps no profession is so geared to making its leader a working machine. But no matter how diligent the effort, the result is never quite satisfactory. Most ministers rarely go home with the satisfaction of knowing that all tasks have been completed. There are always phone calls to return, hospital visits to make, staff meetings to conduct, counseling sessions to schedule, personnel decisions to discuss, programs to plan, committee meetings to attend, speaking engagements to keep, writing deadlines to fulfill, and the relentless need to study for those three or four new sermons each week. And that doesn't include the funerals, weddings, and unexpected crises that are just part of the ministry.

Many ministers are entrepreneurial types. That is, they think beyond their own local church to the broader kingdom of God and perceive the many goals that can be reached. Just as successful businesspeople open branch offices, entrepreneurial ministers use the church as a command center for other avenues of service. Spreading the Gospel is their mission, so they naturally design multiple agencies with which to accomplish that mission: radio, television, print, education, and an endless list of para-church ministries.

Ministers are rarely held accountable for the amount of work they accomplish—unless they are lazy, and the few who fall into that category are usually fired. The ambitious minister with an entrepreneurial instinct is accountable only for his assigned church work. If the church is growing, his board will rarely object to adding new programs. If the pastor feels burdened of the Lord to start a new phase of Christian work and add it to the church's agenda, the board normally approves it. It does not think to ask, "Pastor, who is going to supervise it?" Everyone knows *he* will. And where does the time come from—his family, his marriage, and his personal life.

New ministries are springing up all over the country, a good sign that Christianity is well and ministering to an ever-increasing number of people. But if the person who leads these ministries is not careful, they can soon weave a web of wholesome activity that allows little time to spend with his wife, family, and friends. A minister can extend himself only so long—and then he may cease to be effective. His devotional time begins to suffer. He becomes weary with overwork. He feels guilty at the way he neglects his wife and family. And if he isn't careful, he loses the emotional bond with his wife.

Workaholics like to be considered workaholics, and their egos force them to live up to their reputation for work— no matter what the cost. One of the clearest symptoms of workaholism is that a minister can't relax even when the moment for recreation is extended. Everyone needs time off, even ministers. As Dr. Vance Havner used to say, "If you don't come apart, you will come apart."

Most workaholic ministers will ultimately face burnout. The symptoms of burnout arouse anxiety and dismay in a pastor, because the things that once gave him pleasure— preaching, studying, counseling, ministering, and administrating—begin to become a drag. When that happens, he feels defeated spiritually. And unless he and his wife are very careful, it can tarnish the sparkle of their relationship, which naturally will affect their love life. Richard Exley offers this wise observation:

> When a minister overinvests in his work for an extended period of time, at least two things happen. First, he distances himself from his wife and family. The relationship that should be at the center of his being gets shoved to the ragged edge. His marriage gets the leftovers, the scraps at the end of a demanding day, hardly the stuff of which meaningful marriages are made. And when his marriage is not in good repair, it goes without saying that he is susceptible to an affair. Following MacDonald's resignation he was asked what he had done to restore his marriage relationship. He replied, "It's not as much finding things to do as it is *taking the necessary time*, because for people in ministry, the work is never over."
>
> Which brings us to the second consequence—he wears out! MacDonald said, ". . . I was desperately weary

in spirit and in body." Consequently, when he struggles with temptation, he has neither the inner strength nor the relational resources to resist. He succumbs, I think, oftentimes more out of an inner emptiness than any evil desire.

Let me share an insight which has been helpful to me. The first clue to burnout, and the spiritual and emotional exhaustion which accompanies it, is a lack of inner fulfillment. By experience, I have discovered that I can remain publicly effective long past the point where my work has ceased to be inwardly fulfilling. In fact, I can continue to minister with surprising proficiency even as I begin to resent my work and the very people I am called to serve. If I ignore this warning signal, serious trouble is dead ahead. If, on the other hand, I heed this early warning and take the steps necessary to bring my life back into balance, I can soon return to the ministry with a renewed enthusiasm.[6]

During a time like this, the burned-out minister needs to get away for a protracted time with God, his family, and particularly his wife. He needs to be free from pressure and the everlasting tyranny of responsibility. Unfortunately, that may not be possible, or if it is, he may be too proud to accept it.

Workaholism and burnout can gradually whittle away a minister's inner strength, making him vulnerable to moral collapse. Some men, still functioning long after they are burned out, find an exciting diversion in an available woman. You can imagine the results.

One fallen minister said that he felt so overworked and overextended that he almost yearned for an excuse to get off his self-imposed merry-go-round of activities. Having an affair for him was a way out.

Many churches are beginning to recognize the need for accountability and church-imposed rest times. Sensitive board members can do a lot to help bring balance to a workaholic or burned-out pastor's life. They can make sure the pastor uses vacation time for rest and recreation rather than speaking at a conference or leading a tour to the Holy Land or returning to graduate school. They can insist that just before or after a building program, an extended project, or a particularly difficult time, the pastor take a three-month furlough for rest and recuperation. In my opinion, burnout is like battle fatigue and should be treated in the ministry as it is in the military.

Pastor Bill Hybels, in his message *The Character Crisis*, tells of receiving a letter that illustrates the effects of emotional and physical burnout.

> "Let me state my position on the matter of your needing to slow down." (He was talking to me.) And he said, "I think I have a better-than-average perspective, based on my past experience of ten years as a pastor, five years as a conference speaker. For most of those years I preached or taught over three hundred times a year. I know the incessant demand to deliver material that first would be true, and then be moving and witty and sometimes eloquent. I know that every waking moment for me was spent, one way or another, engaged in amassing material for sermons. Add to this counseling, personal witnessing, administrative responsibilities of running a church, and you have an overly full schedule.
>
> "With all of this, I found myself missing (or conveniently overlooking or justifying) growing signs of problems in my home. Cries for help from my family were drowned out by the roar of the demands of fulfilling my holy calling. When the cries ceased, I assumed the problem had been solved, but it was only that a death had occurred in my relationship with my wife. She now preferred a fantasy relationship with an imaginary lover over the real one she had with me. When I found out there was another man in her life, I was crushed. When the divorce came, I was shattered.
>
> "For seven long years I never preached or taught. The voice that had ministered to thousands was silenced. The ministry that had won hundreds to Christ, by his grace, was terminated. In those days, Bill, I know of no flaw in my devotion to Jesus. There was no extent to which my zeal for him was not willing to go. I was

determined that the gifts God gave me would be used full bore.

"However, Bill, here's my point: Satan shrewdly turned my strengths into my weaknesses. In my zeal to serve the Lord and effectively use the gifts that he gave me, everything else was viewed as competition and at cross-purposes with the goal I was consumed by. Please, I plead with you, don't let this happen to you. Spend time away from the demands of leadership. When someone points the finger of stinging criticism at you for being away from leadership, think of me. Determine you will not let your ministry and your dreams come crashing down around you like mine did around me."

That is sobering, isn't it? The man says, "There's no flaw in my devotion to Jesus." It's that he wore the mantle of leadership too long without help, without enough breaks, and it led him to a point of meltdown and flameout where he made poor decisions, and it cost him everything. There are psychological explanations for why some leaders make bad decisions and end up going wrong ways. It's not necessarily that they're wicked people. It's just that they should have monitored or managed their lives better and taken breaks so that meltdown and flameout didn't happen.[7]

EXTREME SITUATIONS THAT LEAD TO SEXUAL SIN

I feel that no chapter like this one is complete without a brief mention of several other situations that lead to extreme sexual sin. In a way, I wish I didn't have to talk about these situations; they are not pleasant. But my many years in the pastoral and counseling ministry have taught me that many more ministers than we would like to admit live in the worlds I am about to describe. Such men should never have gone into the ministry.

Uncontrolled Lust

We in the church do ourselves no favors by putting our heads in the sand and pretending some of our pastoral leaders do not have serious problems with lust. One minister, the son of a fundamentalist preacher, admitted to having affairs with twenty women before his church fired him and his wife divorced him.

The first time I was brought into a situation of this sort, I was chosen to break the bad news to the minister's wife. I was so young and naïve that I didn't anticipate her reaction. Instead of thanking me for my forthrightness and tact, she attacked me as a liar and troublemaker. Even when she was confronted with irrefutable evidence, she refused to face the truth—that her husband was a three-time loser. Actually, he was a ten-time loser. After he left his church, a friend of mine became his successor. Two years later, he confided to me that "seven married women in this church have come in for counseling. They all carried a guilt complex over having an affair with the former pastor, and none knew about the others." By comparing notes, we discovered that none of the seven he discovered were among the three I could identify.

But the story doesn't end there. Through the years I found three other ministers' wives who claimed he had propositioned them, two of whom rejected him. Twenty-five years later I heard that he had been fired from his last church. When I asked why he had been fired, I was told, "The elders discovered he was having an affair with two women in the church"—the pastor was sixty years old!

Such a man should never have gone into the ministry in the first place. And that is one reason I'm no longer interested in concealing the moral sins of ministers until they are brought under accountability. Unless exposed, they may just continue to use the ministry as an arena to fulfill their lust. Any Christian woman who has succumbed to the charms of this type of minister ought to expose him—at least to his board. Otherwise, he will wreak havoc everywhere he goes, leaving behind not only a trail of emotionally scarred women but, in some cases, broken marriages.

Pornography Addiction

When ministers are addicted to pornography, it is just a matter of time until they destroy their ministry—not to mention their unsuspecting victims. If I seem intolerant, it is because of my frustration at seeing several men I knew personally, men whose talents I greatly admired, ruin themselves and bring reproach to the cause of Christ because of their addiction to pornography.

I am reminded of a minister who had phenomenal talent. If ever a pastor should have succeeded in the ministry, it was this man. However, three times during his ministry he was exposed for reading pornography. Years later, one of his former churches was torn down; in it was found a pile of old pornography magazines dating to the period of his pastorate. What a waste!

Several years ago *Leadership* magazine printed a moving story of a minister who acknowledged a long-term problem with pornography. He maintains that after he repented, the first giant step he needed to make toward deliverance was to confess his sin to someone he respected, someone who would hold him accountable. He then recounted the incredible response he received when he confessed his sin to one of his heroes in the ministry:

> Exactly three days later, I spent the night with a very dear friend, a pastor of one of the largest churches in the South. I had never shared intimate details of my lust life with anyone before, but the schizophrenia was building to such a point I felt I must. He listened quietly, with compassion and great sensitivity, as I recounted a few incidents, skipping over those that showed me in the worst light, and described some of my fears to him.
>
> He sat for a long time with sad eyes after I had finished speaking. We both watched our freshly refilled cups of coffee steam, then stop steaming, then grow cold. I waited for his words of advice or comfort or healing or something. I needed a priest at that moment, someone to say, "Your sins are forgiven."

But my friend was no priest. He did something I never expected. His lip quivered at first, the skin on his face began twitching, and finally he started sobbing—great, huge, wretched sobs, such as I had seen only at funerals.

In a few moments, when he had recovered some semblance of self-control, I learned the truth. My friend was not sobbing for me; he was sobbing for himself. He began to tell me of his own expedition with lust. He had been where I was—five years before. Since that time, he had taken lust to its logical consequences. I will not dwell on sordid details, but my friend had tried it all: bondage, prostitution, bi-sexualism, orgies. He reached inside his vest pocket and pulled out a pad of paper showing the prescriptions he took to fight the venereal disease and anal infections he had picked up along the way. He carries the pad with him on trips, he explained, to buy the drugs in cities where he is anonymous.

I saw my friend dozens of times after that and learned every horrific detail of his hellish life. I worried about cognitive dissonance; he brooded on suicide. I read about deviance; he performed it. I winced at subtle fissures in my marriage; he was in divorce litigation.

I could not sit in judgment on this man, because he had simply ended up where my own obsession would likely take me. Jesus brought together lust and adultery, hatred and murder, in the Sermon on the Mount, not to devalue adultery and murder but rather to point to the awesome truth about hatred and lust. There is a connection.

If I had learned about my friend's journey to debauchery in an article like this one, I doubtless would have clucked my tongue, questioned *Leadership*'s judgment in printing it, and rejected the author as an insincere poseur in the faith. But I knew this man, I thought, as well as I knew anyone. His insights, compassion, and love were all more mature than mine. My sermons were like freshman practice runs compared to his. He was a godly man if I had ever met one, but underneath all that . . . my inner fear jumped uncontrollably. I sensed the power of evil.

For some weeks I lived under a cloud that combined the feelings of doom and terror. Had I crossed some invisible line so that my soul was stained forever? Would I too, like my trusted friend, march inexorably toward the systematic destruction of my body and my soul? He had cried for forgiveness, and deliverance, and every other prayer he had learned in church, and yet now he had fallen into an abyss. Already lawyers were dividing up his house and possessions and his children. Was there no escape for him—for me?[8]

Good news follows in the wake of this depressing article. The author did gain victory from the binding addiction of pornography. Quite possibly the awful revelation of his friend's sin and tragic destruction gave him that added incentive to confess his addiction to his wife and enlist her help, along with God's, in gaining that victory. Five years later he wrote an update on his progress entitled, "The War Within Continues," again anonymously. He stated that his secret to victory was confession to another human being who would hold him accountable.

He is one of the few who have found freedom. I have discovered that victory over pornography addiction is extremely rare. Most victims are reluctant to admit it to their marriage partner, the closest person on earth to them and the one best able to hold them accountable.

Homosexuality

One of my minister friends died of AIDS this year. And while the press quoted him as saying it was contracted through a blood transfusion, hardly any of his friends believed his account. Like many homosexuals, he was a skilled liar. One time right after he had been publicly accused of propositioning a service man, he looked me straight in the eye and insisted, "There was no truth in it." Thus he deceived the Christian community for many years, even though he was almost exposed many times. Such a man should never have entered the ministry until he faced his sin and sought professional help and accountability. But like others driven by this passion, he refused to face it and seek help, hiding it, he thought, from his friends and associates.

The drive for respectability, particularly among Christian homosexuals, is immense. That is why the ministry is so appealing to them. If they can become pastors, missionaries, or youth workers—leading people to Christ and making a significant contribution to his kingdom—their self-doubt and disgust may be allayed. In actuality, however, anyone afflicted with this unnatural sexual drive should never consider the ministry until his perverse drive is truly repented of and forsaken—and even then only after a lengthy probationary period and a willingness to submit to accountability.

IN SUMMARY

Most ministers will face sexual temptation. And if they have not safeguarded their lives in several important areas, they will be vulnerable to those temptations. If the vulnerable minister lets his mind entertain illicit sexual fantasies, his lust gradually rises until the dam of control breaks. The Scripture says that "when lust hath conceived, it bringeth forth sin" (James 1:15 kjv).

That does not mean that the power of Jesus Christ is not sufficient to overcome illicit sexual drives. But because the sex drive is so awesomely powerful, particularly in men, ministers need to be constantly on guard, protecting their lives from these vulnerabilities. And the rest of us need to help them safeguard their lives by providing loving accountability.

CHAPTER 4

The Real Reason Ministers Fall

*A*lthough the factors described in the last chapter all can contribute to a minister's fall, none of them is the bottom line. The bottom line is *sin*. Plain, old-fashioned sin.

We can blame pride, an aggressive woman, an unresponsive wife, workaholism, or a dozen other factors, but if we are honest, we must admit that a minister falls because he wants to. No one forces him to get into bed with a woman other than his wife. Let's face it, a man can't be raped! He is always a cooperative participant.

Most falls are not one-time sexual experiences but affairs that have gone on for months or years. A fallen minister is rarely guilty of single acts of uncontrolled passion. As we have seen, his fall may have been the result of a long-term association with a Christian woman with whom he finds more emotional bonding than he does with his wife. Once the other woman replaces his wife emotionally, it is only a matter of time before she also supplants her physically.

WHATEVER HAPPENED TO THE "EXCEEDING SINFULNESS OF SIN"?

Modern society's permissive attitude no longer recognizes adultery as a sin. A recent Harvard University study of human sexuality indicates that "50 percent of the married men" and "40 percent of the married women have had extramarital affairs."[1]

The church, however, has never based its morality on the world's standards. The Bible hasn't changed—adultery still is and always will be wrong! But somehow we have lost the keen awareness of what one of my late Bible teachers, Dr. Wilbur Smith, used to call "the exceeding sinfulness of sin."

GOD'S LOVE REPLACES GOD'S JUDGMENT

During the past forty years, our churches have emphasized "God's love" at the expense of "God's judgment." Perhaps as a reaction to the legalistic emphasis of fundamentalism during the first half of this century, Christians felt the need to emphasize, especially to the lost, Dr. Bill Bright's expression, "God loves you and has a wonderful plan for your life." While that principle is true, we should never lose sight of the fact that God is also just. He holds us accountable to live righteous lives.

After a minister is exposed for the sin of adultery, Christians who love that minister may entreat, "Shouldn't we forgive him and let him go right on preaching?"—as if no moral law has been broken.

We can't allow ourselves to become blind to the seriousness of sin. God hates sin, and so should we. Dr. G. Raymond Carlson, the leader of the Assemblies of God church, was inundated with critical letters from those who loved Jimmy Swaggart and felt that his church leaders were too severe in requiring that he stay out of public ministry for one year after his sin was made public. Many of the letters asked, "Doesn't the New Testament teach forgiveness?" "If God can forgive his sin, why can't we?" That is a good question—and there is an appropriate answer. Forgiveness, in contrast to restoration, is instantaneous the moment a person sincerely confess his or her sins. Restoration, on the other hand, takes *time*—time for the sinner to rebuild his life and time for others to rebuild their trust in the sinner.

All adulterers or sex offenders can be instantly forgiven when they repent in the name of Jesus Christ, as 1 John 1:7–9 makes abundantly clear. But that doesn't permit a fallen leader who has proven he is *not* morally trustworthy to regain his position of moral and spiritual leadership. He must *re-prove* himself—to his wife, his community, the church, and the Lord. Our Lord announced a fundamental principle of judgment when he said: "From everyone who has been given much, much will be demanded; and from the one who has been entrusted with much, much more will be asked" (Luke 12:48).

SEXUAL SINS ARE GREATER THAN OTHER SINS

The Bible places a high priority on sexual faithfulness, and the punishment for sexual sin reflects that priority. The Bible requires a greater punishment for sexual sins than for any other sin except for renouncing the Lord and murder. There are three primary reasons for such a distinction.

First, God designed the sex act to be a sacred function that gives to mankind a godlike gift: procreation. Only God can create life—except in what I like to call *the act of marriage*. When a husband and wife, with the blessing of God, express their love for each other sexually and in the process create another human being with an eternal soul, a free will, and the capacity to pass that gift on to the next generation, they are using a sacred gift that should never be used illegitimately.

Several ministers who have had more than one extramarital affair probably never would have repeated their offense if the first sin had been dealt with scripturally. One Christian counselor kept the knowledge of a minister's sin to a restricted group of four people, which did not include the minister's wife. The minister repented but was reprimanded so lightly that a few years later he fell again. He wasn't so fortunate on that occasion, for his sexual sin was made public, and now the entire body of Christ knows about it. The counselor was remiss in not forcing the man to confess his sin to his wife—for three reasons: (1) he would have been faced more directly with the severity of his sin; (2) his wife would have been able to hold him more accountable in the future; and (3) the embarrassing confrontation may have prompted them to work out any sexual deficiencies that may have existed between them.

Second, sexual sins are greater than other sins because they have always been a significant target of attack by Satan. Most of the false religions of the world include sexual violations of God's laws as part of their religious observances. These sexual practices, even when done in the name of religion, have so weakened nations by disease, pollution, and death that some of these nations are extinct. Many Bible scholars believe that God's mandate to exterminate the Canaanites was given because the entire nation was riddled by venereal disease; a severe measure was necessary to protect the Israelites, the future inhabitants of the land, from pollution.

Third, the Old Testament lists only six capital offenses— that is, six crimes for which people were condemned to be stoned to death. Two of them were sexual sins: adultery (or fornication) and homosexuality. Nowhere in the Bible did God require death for liars or truce-breakers. But he did require execution for those who had sexual involvement with people other than their marriage partners.

While today's rationalists reject such extreme measures as "inhumane," they have created such a permissive society that far more human suffering is caused by their refusal to execute sexual offenders than if they had maintained God's fidelity laws. Nowhere is that more apparent than in the AIDS epidemic. Authorities suspect that AIDS was brought to America by one Canadian airline steward who was involved with several homosexual partners. Already more innocent victims of polluted blood transfusions have died than if the steward's life had been taken for committing a capital offense. Even more futile is the secular humanist's refusal to permit contact tracing of homosexuals or to pass laws that forbid homosexuals to give blood transfusions, which already have caused the disease to spread and many innocent victims to die. Sexual sins are far more serious than we are led to believe today—and part of the reason is the silence of the church in condemning them.

ADULTERY IS A SPIRITUAL PROBLEM

Adultery is first and foremost a spiritual problem, particularly for a minister. I may be criticized for being too simplistic in making that statement, but it is true neverthe-less. God has promised that "he will not let you be tempted beyond what you can bear. But when you are tempted, he will also provide a way out so that you can stand up under it" (1 Cor. 10:13b). Consequently, either God has failed the fallen minister, or the minister has sinned with his eyes wide open. Since God can't fail, we must learn to "flee youthful lusts" and deal with temptation *quickly*. If the truth were known, the Lord probably had opened several avenues of escape from sexual temptation for each minister who fell.

It is important to understand that sin originates in the mind and is forwarded to the emotions, which fuel the body. The safeguard of the mind is the spirit, which is why Scripture tells us "sin shall not be your master" (Rom. 6:14a). Our spirit protects the mind—if we want it to.

The following diagram is one of the best concepts God

Graphic 1

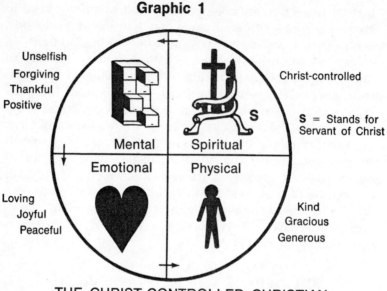

Unselfish
Forgiving
Thankful
Positive

Christ-controlled

S = Stands for
Servant of Christ

Mental | Spiritual

Emotional | Physical

Loving
Joyful
Peaceful

Kind
Gracious
Generous

THE CHRIST-CONTROLLED CHRISTIAN

has given me for understanding ourselves and for helping us to realize the resources he has made available to us. It is based on the command of Christ, "Love the Lord your God with all your *heart* and with all your *soul* and with all your *strength* and with all your *mind*" (Luke 10:27, emphasis added). When considered in the light of other passages, such as "Out of [the heart] spring the issues of life" (Prov. 4:23 NKJV), "As [a man] thinks in his heart, so is he" (Prov. 23:7 NKJV) and "Take captive every thought to make it obedient to Christ" (2 Cor. 10:5), we can draw the following concept for living.

Human nature includes four aspects: the mind, heart, soul, and body. All are commanded to "love God." Trouble comes when I direct that love toward someone or something else. My *will* is the seat of my soul, where God's Spirit comes to dwell when I receive Jesus Christ by faith. Salvation is actually a surrender of my will to Christ as Lord of my life. As long as I subordinate my thoughts to Christ, I can control my emotions, which, in turn, are like the motor of my life, producing the "issues of life," or the activities of the body.

The following diagram shows two married people in love—"ideal compatibility." This couple is well matched spiritually, mentally, emotionally, and physically.

Graphic 2

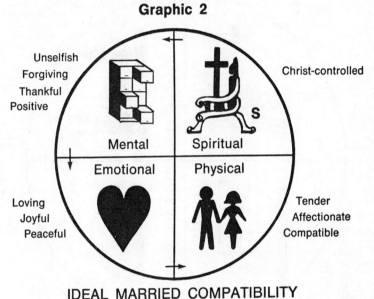

IDEAL MARRIED COMPATIBILITY

Now suppose something slowly destroys their mental compatibility—perhaps a young wife becomes burdened with small children or the husband becomes busy with church activities or she goes through menopause or he experiences a mid-life crisis. Or he develops a mental compatibility with another woman. If the husband and this other woman are thrown together at work, they may cultivate more common areas of thought life than he and his wife enjoy. If he doesn't bring those thoughts into captivity to Christ, before long he will be entertaining romantic thoughts

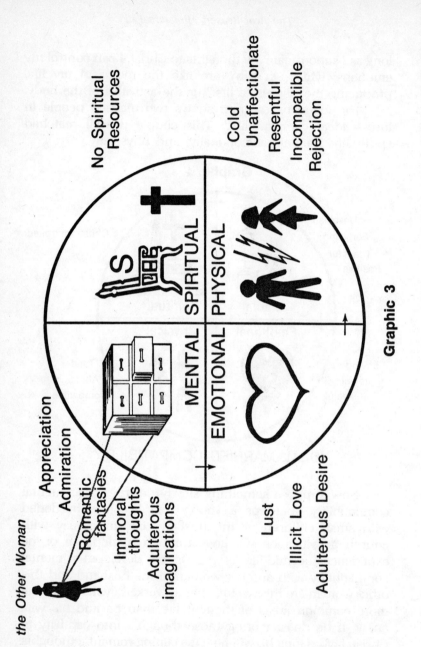

the Other Woman

Appreciation
Admiration

Romantic
fantasies

Immoral
thoughts

Adulterous
imaginations

MENTAL   SPIRITUAL

No Spiritual
Resources

EMOTIONAL   PHYSICAL

Cold
Unaffectionate
Resentful
Incompatible
Rejection

Lust
Illicit Love
Adulterous Desire

Graphic 3

that ignite his emotions. If such considerations are not reserved for his wife, they will grieve the spiritual side of his nature, which will look like the facing-page illustration.

Obviously, this minister's sin didn't start in bed with the other woman. It began with reflections about her— reflections that, according to God, should have been reserved for his wife.

The minister need not be blind to the quality and personality of women with whom he works, but he shouldn't "love them with his mind." For example, I can look at a new car, admiring it, approving it with my eyes. But when I start to "love" it—even though I don't own it or can't afford it—my "love" becomes lust. It's amazing how I can become cool toward a car when I begin to think about the payments I can't afford—even while I approve of the car. Similarly, a man may approve of and even admire a woman who isn't his wife, but since she is *not* his wife, he must not "love" her.

Be sure of this: no man will love God with all his heart, mind, soul, and strength—and at the same time love a woman who is not his wife. If a man loves God as he should, romantic thoughts and emotions will be reserved for his wife. When sexual thoughts about another woman enter his mind, they should be blocked by stern messages of reproof: "Forbidden!" "The result leads to disaster!" "Displeasing to Christ!" As a friend reminded me, "No man ever jumped into bed with another woman while he sang, 'Oh, how I love Jesus'!"

I can understand when a minister sins. He loves Jesus the majority of the time, for most of his life—but the exception defeats him. My friends who have fallen into sexual sin are not evil, degenerate men. They have been godly leaders most of their lifetime, but a few brief interludes tripped them up. As much as it grieves me to say this, during the times of their adultery, they were living in *sin*. To their credit, the fallen men I know admit that they were enduring a hell on earth, torn between guilt and cries of repentance.

Think of it this way: the Christian life is compared to a race. We have all watched the runners who ran successfully nine-tenths of the way around the track, but that doesn't ensure victory. You can't win unless the entire race is run properly. The man who guards his thought life will never sin with his body. Conversely, the man who sins with his body, whether it be adultery or any other sin, has long before sinned with his mind. Had he confessed those illegitimate thoughts to a trusted friend before they led to emotional bonding with a woman who was not his wife, he probably would have saved his ministry, marriage, and integrity.

Whenever a minister falls, evaluators may quickly identify "a deep-rooted psychological problem" that caused him to act in an immoral manner and "make bad choices." That's nonsense! He had a sin problem. The sooner we face that fact, the sooner we can begin helping him put his life back together. Like everyone else, ministers sin because they are sinners who didn't look to God in their hour of temptation. Instead, they continued to entertain the temptation. Adultery is the result of choice, a sin-motivated choice. But the good news is that the adultery can be forgiven. Whether its effects can be forgotten remains to be seen.

One of my minister friends had an absolutely wretched relationship with his wife, a selfish shrew who dealt out sexual relations for good behavior. He sinned initially by indulging in self-pity. While we can understand his thought process, from a spiritual vantage point it can't be defended, for it set him up for depression. Concluding that his marriage was hopeless, he was drawn to an equally troubled married woman in his congregation. After several counseling sessions, they met for lunch—followed by walks in the park. Because of their mutual commitment to living a holy life, their relationship was simply one of mutual friendship for a long time. The sincerity of that friendship made their unhappy marriages more livable "for their children's sake."

Whether or not they realized it, their mental bonding

led to emotional bonding, and it was only a matter of time before their relationship became sexual. First it was holding hands, then a parting kiss, then protracted kissing—and you can imagine the rest. Both claimed that they sincerely didn't want their relationship to become sexual. Unfortunately, they and scores of others don't realize that they were making "provision for the flesh" (Rom. 13:14 NKJV). You can't trust the flesh! The path from mental to emotional to physical bonding reflects the normal course of human nature.

When should they have taken the way of escape? When they recognized their dangerous mental bonding. When one's inner being admits, "I have more in common with you than I do with my married partner," that is a warning sign! At certain stages of marital disunity and times of low spiritual ebb, almost anyone can stumble into such an alliance—particularly ministers, who are thrown into intimate relationships with so many women, some of whom don't have fulfilling marriages. To remain pure, a minister must avoid all such contacts or keep them totally at a professional level. One earnest pastor admitted, "When I find myself bonding with a woman in counseling, I pass her on to a colleague or share the temptation with one of my staff men, who will hold me accountable for my behavior." Obviously, he doesn't trust his flesh.

When a relationship becomes excessively emotional, it is almost too late to stop it, short of outside help. We are all such emotional creatures that if we cultivate our emotions even a little, we are vulnerable to sin—even if that means violating our moral principles. Most people don't understand that emotions are stronger than the will. Whenever the will and emotions enter into conflict, we can almost be certain that the emotions will win. For that reason we must label sins of the mind for what they are and *stop* them while the will is still in control. If we wait until our emotions take charge, it will be too late. The pastor who brings every thought into captivity to Christ will not commit adultery because he will retain emotional control. The minister who agrees to meet a tempting counselee or woman friend in a clandestine place, even for lunch, is playing with fire.

One fallen minister should be a tragic warning to all of us. When his sin was discovered, he was fired from his church as well as disgraced in the eyes of his family, friends, and community. Then his wife seized the occasion to divorce him and convinced the court to give her the children. His sexual partner returned to her unhappy marriage. Today the ex-minister is a lonely, broken, and pathetic figure, trying vainly to find some place where he can serve the Lord he betrayed. Would to God that tempted ministers could meet and talk with such a man *before* they fall into adultery! No sexual sin is worth the price a minister pays when he is exposed.

One minister says this about his period of misery: "I will never forget those first days. It was almost impossible to ward off the feeling that life was over, that all the brightness and joy that we had known for more than forty-five years had come to a screeching halt. But those are feelings, and they move quickly into one of the most dangerous moods: self-pity."

This pastor goes on to explain how he and his wife gradually were led out of this misery to a point of peace and rebuilding, but not all fallen pastors find that relief. Many ministers feel suicidal during the first months after their fall. So far, I have not yet found one who actually took his own life, but the pain for most is almost severe enough to make him do so.

Of all the men I have talked to who endured this experience, each one has sworn he will die before committing that sin again—and he means it. However, if he doesn't win the sin battle while it is still in his mind, he will once again become vulnerable to the flesh.

CHAPTER 5

How to Avoid Sexual Temptation

*M*inisters are first and foremost men—so don't be surprised if they act and react like men. They face enormous temptation because they work closely with many women, entering into a sacred intimacy zone in counseling or ministry. The danger of that trust shouldn't be ignored; ministers should take extra precautions to avoid the resultant temptations.

STEP ONE: WALK IN THE SPIRIT

So I say, live by the Spirit, and you will not gratify the desires of the sinful nature. For the sinful nature desires what is contrary to the Spirit, and the Spirit what is contrary to the sinful nature. They are in conflict with each other, so that you do not do what you want. But if you are led by the Spirit, you are not under law (Gal. 5:16–18).

Next to being sexual creatures, ministers are also spiritual beings. If they heed Paul's command, they will not be overcome by lust that leads to adultery. One can't walk in lust and in the Spirit at the same time. We have already seen that adultery starts in the mind, and thus before it ignites the emotional sin of lust, it has grieved the Spirit. Temptations to sin in the mind are everywhere. A minister must always be on his guard to maintain a pure mind lest he commit adultery in his heart (Matt. 5:28). While the consequences of heart adultery aren't nearly as severe as physical adultery, if indulged long enough, thought will inevitably lead to action.

Walking in the Spirit mentally will at times demand all the self-control a pastor can muster. The good news is that self-control is one of the nine fruits of the Spirit. However, a minister can negate that control by surrendering his mind to lust-producing sights and thoughts, which often inundate him after his greatest spiritual experiences. But if he really wants to maintain a godly mind, he must anticipate temptations in advance and establish a battle strategy to guarantee their defeat.

I remember the first time I stumbled onto pornographic programming while flipping the TV dial in a hotel room. I had just spoken at a conference where God had moved powerfully. Tired and attempting to catch the evening news, I was suddenly confronted with a sex scene that should be illegal to send over the formerly "federally controlled air waves." I had to provide my own control. I didn't! And suddenly I found my emotions running away with me—*after* I had grieved the Holy Spirit.

That experience taught me a valuable lesson. I made a commitment to God and myself that I would apply to TV the same policy that I have long observed regarding print pornography. I never look at it. Now when I accidentally turn to a channel that is broadcasting pornography, I instantly flip the switch. Frankly, I enjoy the feeling of approval I get from not grieving the Holy Spirit. Moral purity comes only through constant vigilance. If you never grieve the Spirit with your mind, you will never grieve him with your body.

STEP TWO: RESPECT SEXUAL TEMPTATION

Some of my friends succumbed to moral failure largely because they didn't respect the power of sexual temptation. Almost all said in effect, "I can't believe I could ever have done such a thing" or "I never dreamed it would happen to me."

Sexual sins have always been temptation number one, particularly for men. In Galatians 5:19–21, after commanding us to "walk in the Spirit," the apostle Paul catalogued eighteen sins of the flesh. It is no accident that the first four are sexual sins: adultery, fornication, uncleanness, and lasciviousness. All over the world and throughout all human history, sexual temptation has led the list. And the Christians who think they are immune to the effects of that temptation have, in my opinion, already taken the first step in its direction.

A minister must always recognize that he can't trust his flesh; he must *regularly* be on guard against sexual temptation. Don't trust the flesh as long as you live. The seventy-year-old counseling pastor who was having affairs with two women ought to remind us of that.

STEP THREE: CULTIVATE YOUR MARRIAGE RELATIONSHIP

Develop a Warm Sexual Relationship with Your Wife

The Bible is amazingly frank about one of the purposes of marriage when it warns, "It is better to marry than to burn with passion" (1 Cor. 7:9). Very few men can live without sexual involvement. God provided marriage to satisfy the sex drive, one of his special gifts to us. When marriage partners withhold themselves from each other, they intensify their partner's temptation.

Whenever I counsel couples after one of them has committed adultery, I hear most of them affirm, "We have always had a good sex life." Wives are prone to claim that more than husbands.

Then I ask, "How many times a week did you make love during the two months before the affair?" The answers range anywhere from once or twice a month to once a week. Never have I heard "three times a week" for couples in their thirties to fifties, although that is the national average. It is my guess that few if any of ministers who had extramarital sexual involvements were having satisfying sex with their wife three times a week.

Unfortunately, when a wife feels her husband's affection waning and becomes suspicious, she often withdraws from her husband sexually. That is her first mistake! A godly, loving wife who is wise enough to be suspicious of her husband's alienation of affection should forget her pride and disappointment, becoming more aggressive sexually as a contribution to preserving her home, marriage, and ministry. Every wife of a fallen minister laments that she did not do this— after it is too late. Typically, some return his lack of ardor with coolness, thinking such things as, "He wouldn't dare be unfaithful; he made a sexual commitment to me when we married." She is right, but that attitude will not lessen his temptation the way lovemaking will.

One minister friend who travels a lot shared this intimate secret with me as we discussed the tragic fall of some of our friends. He and his wife enjoyed a warm, loving relationship for many years, even though he was usually the sexual aggressor. His wife was usually very responsive, but she rarely initiated their love experiences—with one regular exception. The last day before he left on a preaching trip, he could tell that she was interested in making love. "No matter how preoccupied I would get in preparing for the trip, we almost always made love the night before or the morning I left town." He then added, "And she usually initiated it." She is a wise and loving wife.

Keep Your Love Life Romantic

Married couples tend to make the common mistake of gradually taking their love life for granted. Naturally, their physical relationship will not be as exciting after thirty years as it was on the honeymoon. But it can be more fulfilling and meaningful. Honeymooners are usually more interested in quantity than quality. That may last for six months or a year, but gradually the frequency of their intercourse level diminishes. When it is limited to two or three times a week, it can be the culmination of many expressions of love, all of which build toward the most exciting experience two people can share on this earth.

It is important that married ministers be good lovers—which requires that they understand women. They should be more aware of women's needs than most men, of course, because they have studied the subject, consulted with couples before marriage, and heard women in counseling share feelings that most men never hear. Such intimate knowledge of women should enable a minister to meet his wife's needs.

Men need to know that women are different from men not only physically but also emotionally and psychologically. Most good women don't like sex just for the sake of sex. Men can enjoy sex as a physical experience; women usually feel cheated unless "romance" is involved. Wives frequently complain in the counseling room, "The only time my husband shows interest in love is when he wants sex." Women don't like to be used as sex objects; they prefer to be loved as persons, with sex serving as the culmination of the relationship. And even then they expect some affection during the "afterglow."

A wise husband romances his wife from the time he comes home until bedtime. Of course, that has to be done more subtly as the children mature, but he can speak endearingly to her and respectfully of her. Even helping around the house can say, "I love you." Most women respond warmly to kindness, graciousness, respect, and thoughtful leadership. I have observed that particularly in love-starved women who had an affair. It wasn't passion or a sex drive that found them in another man's bed; it was their longing for the "ness" needs: tenderness, thoughtfulness, kindness. Christian husbands are commanded to provide all of these, the very elements that produce emotional bonding and the best married lovemaking.

Make Your Marriage a Priority

"Married strangers" or "estranged partners" still living together do not as a rule experience exciting sex. They may go through the motions and provide "due benevolence," which may be better than nothing, but that is about all. When that happens, the culprit is usually a lack of meaningful time spent together.

All couples face a natural enemy to their sex life: the contrasting inner clocks for expressing physical love. A man is prone to be quick and hurried, whereas a woman likes to savor the romance of the moment when she has her husband all to herself. A wise husband conforms his desire to his wife's need—no matter how pressured his work, no matter how limited his time.

The ministry today is not conducive to a healthy family life and marriage. The many demands on the minister's time at church, the mental effort required to prepare three or four new messages every week, and the countless interferences at home—all disrupt normal family life. Many ministers find it difficult to leave their responsibilities at the door and shift their full attention to the needs of a wife and children.

What is the bottom line? Priority. In these pressurized days, all married people must allow marital and family relationships to take priority over other things—even their vocation, if necessary. Unfortunately, many people wait until it is too late before realizing that if they lose their family, nothing else really matters. That is particularly true for ministers. The Bible clearly states that he should be the "husband of one wife"; if his wife leaves him, he has almost no hope to regain a pastoral ministry.

Richard Exley tells the story of a minister whose wife totally closed him out of her life. Instead of blaming her, he recognized that she was reacting to the way he had abandoned her for "the other woman" in his life—his church. A woman is no match for a congregation. Playing servant to his church at the expense of his family can be easily (though erroneously) defended on "spiritual" grounds, but how can a Christian wife tell her husband, "You're spending too much time serving the Lord"? She had better muster the courage to remind him, "You're spending too much time neglecting me and the children." This minister bravely bared his soul for others to see—and hopefully to profit from. When I read it, I wept. I wish every pastor and Christian leader would read this true story.

Church activities frequently require the pastor to attend meetings, of one sort or another, five and six nights a week. As a consequence his marriage suffers, both by his absence, and from exhaustion when he is present. His wife may well feel abandoned, even betrayed. Dr. Dennis Guernsey, author and professor of psychology at Fuller Theological Seminary, says: "A pastor's wife is put in a terrible bind when the church becomes The Other Woman—but her husband isn't unrighteous for sleeping with her. No one considers this obsession immoral; he's 'doing God's work.'"

Yet for the pastor's wife, it can become an open sore, a continuing source of frustration, even resentment. Never have I heard the pain and hopelessness more graphically, more eloquently, expounded than by Walter Wangerin, Jr., author and pastor. He writes:

"What did I learn that Sunday evening in our kitchen when Thanne broke silence and burned me with my guilt? What did I hear from the small woman grown huge in her fury, half in, half out of her coat, while the daylight died outside? I learned her grievances. I heard what her life had been like for several years, though I had not known it. I saw myself through her eyes, and the vision accused me.

"You decide my whole life for me," [Thanne said to me], "but you hardly pay mind to the decisions. You do it with your left hand, carelessly. You run me with your left hand. Everyone else gets the right hand of kindness. Everyone else can talk to you. Not me. The left hand."

"A good pastor!" she spat the words. "You *are a* good pastor, Wally. God knows, I wanted you to be a good pastor. But sometimes I wish you were a bad pastor, a lazy pastor, a careless pastor. Then I'd have a right to complain. Or maybe I'd have *you* here sometimes. A good pastor! Wally, how can I argue with God and take you from Him? Wally, Wally, your ministry runs *me*, but you leave me alone exactly when I need you. *Where are you all the time?*"

Then this is what she told me in the darkening kitchen that terrible Sunday evening. This is what she made me see: that this good pastor carried to the people of his congregation a face full of pity—

—but at our dinner table my face was drained and grey. At the dinner table I heaped a hundred rules upon our children, growling at them for the least infraction. Our dinners were tense and short.

Thanne said she knew how much I hated to visit the jail. But I went. And it never mattered what time of day or night. Yet I did nothing I hated, nothing, at home.

For counseling and for sermons, my words, she said, were beautiful: a poet of the pulpit. But for our bedroom conversations, my words were bitter, complaining, and unconsidered. We talked of my duties. We talked of my pastoral disappointments. Or we hardly talked at all.

I was ministering. I was a whole human, active in an honorable job, receiving the love of a grateful congregation, charging out the door in the mornings, collapsing in bed at night. I was healthy in society; she was dying in a little house—and accusing herself for the evil of wanting more time from me, stealing the time from God. I laughed happily at potlucks. She cried in secret. And sometimes she would simply hold one of the children, would hold and hold him, pleading some little love from him until he grew frightened by her intensity, unable in his babyhood to redeem her terrible sins. And sometimes she cursed herself for burdening a child, and then she wondered where God had gone.

In those days the smile died in her face. The high laughter turned dusty in her throat. Privately the woman withered—and I did not see it. . . .

I said, "We need to be together." I meant that with all my heart. And I continued, "We need to make the time to be together. What I should do," I said—but would this insult Thanne?—"What I should do is make appointments on my calendar for you. Oh, forgive me for sounding so businesslike. But I should write it in my schedule book."

I said, "Every night we'll spend the hour before supper together. I'll be home and we'll talk together. I'll write that in my book. What do you think? That doesn't demean you, does it? Maybe it does. But I'll do it." I said all this to the ceiling. And I said, "We'll spend a weekend together, you and me alone. Two nights, three days, away from home. Count on it. This year, next year, all the years. I'll be with you. I promise you I will."

In the days that followed, I came home before dinner. A full hour before dinner. And I sat on a stool in the kitchen while Thanne cooked. And this is how I felt: artificial. The little talk we made was mostly forced, and Thanne was mostly silent. Well, our lives had been different in the last years, more divergent than we realized; we had little in common after all. Worse, Thanne was simply not sure whether she could trust my care for her or my change. It would be a risky thing to reveal herself to the one who had hurt her and could hurt her yet again. She did love me. She had rediscovered it and told me so. But I don't think we were friends much.

The cup, the daily hour, continued empty for a while.

But even if it was empty, it was *there*. First it had to be that form—and then it might, when the time was right, be filled.

I kept coming home. Even when we didn't talk, I came. It was simple labor, the keeping of a covenant for its own sake, because it had been promised; there is no excitement in this part of the story.

But the mere persistence of the cup caused Thanne to begin to trust it. If I was there yesterday, then I could be there tomorrow—therefore, she might risk a word or two today. And she did. Thanne began to talk. She began to believe that I would listen. And I did. The more she talked, the more I *wanted* to listen, and the more my own talk wasn't merely self-centered.

It is a wonder when your beloved trusts you enough to give herself to you again, trusts you with her weight, her treasure, and her life. In time the cup, which had proven itself, began to fill with the serious liquid of our lives. What a valuable vessel is a cup, a covenant!

Now, though we may be separate in the morning, the ideas that occur to us apart we save for the hour when we will be together, because we trust in that hour; and it is as though we'd been together the whole day through. If Thanne suffers another sin of mine, it needn't swell in secret until it explodes. The cup is there for it, a place for it, and I drink from the cup, both the medicine that wakens and purges me, and the love with which she nourishes me.[1]

I have observed that many women will put up with neglect, anger, contempt, brutality, and even adultery just so long. Then something deep down inside snaps—usually the final reaction to hopeless despair. They lose all assurance that their situation will change. Such women may even be vulnerable for an affair themselves, sometimes just for spite, sometimes to prove to themselves that another man will find them desirable.

Such cases can be remedied, as in the beautiful story above, particularly if caught before a third person becomes involved. But they must take deliberate steps toward a solution, like scheduling regular time on a daily basis. I also recommend mini-honeymoons at least every quarter, scheduled long in advance and protected at all costs. A night and a day in a motel with one's own partner can be an exciting stimulant to any marriage.

Recently I was seated with a young pastor and his wife at a banquet in his church. It didn't take a master detective to notice a troubled relationship. While talking to him, I purposely steered the conversation to some of the material I was including in this book. He was all ears! Then I asked if he and his wife ever took mini-honeymoons together. "We can't afford it!" he grimaced.

Was the pastor's predicament financial? No. I believe he just didn't want to be alone with his wife that long. If he doesn't wise up, his ministry could be in danger.

STEP FOUR: FLEE YOUTHFUL LUSTS

Paul's advice to young Timothy, his son in the faith, to "flee youthful lusts" was probably directed toward a single man (2 Tim. 2:22 NKJV). If the Apostle were alive today and observed the number of married ministers falling into moral sins, I'm confident he would include married men.

Dr. Henrietta C. Mears, an outstanding worker with young people, once said, "I wouldn't trust the best man we have with the wrong woman." Like Paul, she taught men to "flee youthful lusts."

Joseph, one of the Bible's greatest men, protected his moral life at all costs. As you probably remember from his story, when Potiphar's wife tried to entice him into her bed, he fled so fast that he left his cape clutched in her lusting hand.

Be sure of this: every fallen leader now wishes he had fled. Unfortunately, most men think they are able to fend off such provocations. One principle I learned early in my ministry—I can't trust the flesh, particularly mine. That distrust may well have saved me from destroying my ministry and marriage.

Many years ago I held special meetings in a church thirty miles away and drove home each night. A very attractive woman attended regularly and made a point of offering an ego-building observation after each service. I hate to confess it, but I ate it up. One night she invited me over for pie and coffee, saying that her husband was at home. I went, expecting her husband to be there. When I arrived, I saw no husband—or kids. I immediately asked where her husband was, to which she replied, "He just ran out to the store. He will be right back." I had to make a quick decision. Politely excusing myself, I fled! Now the situation may have been perfectly harmless; at best it didn't look good, and at worst it could have been disastrous. I have never regretted that decision, for it cost me nothing—except a piece of pie.

The minister who follows Joseph's example never lives to regret it. The man who protests that he is able to withstand such temptations should heed the words of the apostle Paul, "If you think you are standing firm, be careful that you don't fall" (1 Cor. 10:12).

The man who recognizes that he can't trust his flesh is not likely to cave in to temptation, for he will deal with it the best way he can—and that is to flee.

STEP FIVE: FIDELITY INSURANCE—COUPLE PRAYER

For many years I have advocated that couples develop the habit of praying together before retiring each night or at least four or five nights a week. Praying together not only is a spiritual growth experience for the couple, but it also develops within them a spiritual intimacy. Rarely will a man be unfaithful to the woman he prays with each night. Were he to try, I have a hunch his voice would sound like "sounding brass and tinkling cymbals."

The method of couple prayer that Bev and I have found most enjoyable is an offshoot of conversational prayer. When couple prayer is implemented, on the first night the husband should pray for the major burden of his heart for one to two minutes, then quit and let his wife pray from her vantage point about that same concern. Then he should pray for his second heart burden, followed by her response. When they have covered about five, it's probably time to go to sleep—unless one or both are heavily burdened.

The next night it's the wife's turn to lead with her major burden, followed by her husband's response. If the couple adheres to this procedure four or five nights a week, they will find themselves sharing what they really feel deep down. It is a powerful means of communication that will draw them together like few things I know on this earth. Before long one person will begin to pray about burdens that originally started on the partner's heart, a healthy sign that they are beginning to merge spiritually. This kind of prayer life will enrich almost any marriage and serve as "fidelity insurance" to those who are tempted.

Marriage is somewhat like insurance: we don't really appreciate it until a crisis arises. I am convinced that a large majority of those Christians who have been devastated by a divorce failed to appreciate the delights of a unified marriage until it was too late. Many have admitted, "If I had known how lonely life is without someone to share my life with, I would have worked harder at making a go of it."

And that is my point—a strong marriage relationship takes priority, time, and effort. We get out of it exactly what we put into it. With God's help, when couples treat each other in love and respect, they *can* live happily ever after.

PART II
Can They Be Restored?

CHAPTER 6

What a Church Should Do When Its Minister Falls

*L*osing a pastor or leader in a disgraceful public fall is one of the most devastating experiences a church can endure. Since no one ever anticipates such an event, few churches are prepared when it arises.

The Navy has a term for handling an emergency such as a sudden fire or explosion aboard a ship at sea: damage control. The best way for a church to avoid the trauma that follows tragedy is to prepare a damage-control plan well in advance.

The following plan is designed to minimize the damage for the church, the pastor, and his family. Naturally, variant procedures will be used, based on whether the church intercepted an ongoing affair or confronted a repentant pastor—who had already dealt with his sin privately. A well-established plan will not lessen the harmful publicity that always follows such a tragedy, of course, but it will limit the harmful effects of the sin.

The following model is designed for the kinds of situation with which I'm most familiar: the pastor acknowledges his sin, is repentant, and has discontinued the illicit relationship. In some cases, he may not have told his wife. However, if the pastor denies accusations of immorality, it will, of course, complicate even the following procedure.

1. DISCOVER THE FACTS

Before any action is taken, a small group of board members or elders (not more than six people) should investigate the rumors and confidentially confront the pastor with their findings. Rumors abound today, particularly since the overly publicized televangelist scandals. Before confronting the pastor, church leaders must have their facts in place. If he is innocent, the perpetrators of vicious rumors should be extended appropriate church discipline—for both their sake and as a warning to the whole church. Every effort should be made to determine the truth, for what's at stake is not only a church's reputation but also the pastor's life and career.

One minister was falsely accused of sexual improprieties while he was serving as prayer chairman of the Billy Graham crusade scheduled to start in his city in two weeks. The man was so conscientious that his greatest concern was the possibility that a scandal might negatively impact the crusade. Consequently, he resigned from both the church and the committee. Neither the church nor his ministry were ever the same. He is dead now, but the church is a pathetic shadow of what it was when he served as its pastor. If his board had researched the evidence properly instead of believing false rumors, the body of Christ would not have created unnecessary distress for one of its members.

2. ASK FOR THE MINISTER'S IMMEDIATE RESIGNATION

If the minister truly has been guilty of adultery while pastoring the church, he should be asked to resign and to make a full confession to the official board or elders of the church. The entire congregation doesn't need to know the details or the identity of the sexual partner, but they should be assured that their elected leaders have reviewed the evidence. The church should be spared an emotional public confession. The pastor should write out a resignation that can be read to the congregation. The confession should include an acknowledgment of moral guilt; otherwise those who love him will become defensive and even turn on the leadership, accusing them of persecuting the pastor. Then the church should be called to prayer—for themselves, the pastor, his family, and the cause of Christ.

3. MAKE A FINANCIAL SETTLEMENT WITH THE MINISTER

The elders or board members should grant the minister a financial severance package that will provide care for his family. Under ideal circumstances it is difficult for ministers to move to a new church on short notice; in disgrace it is all but impossible. The congregation, who may not be privy to the details, will want to know that he and his family were dealt with in a Christlike way.

Every church responds differently. Some thoughtlessly give nothing; others offer a month's salary for each year of service to the church. For the man who has conducted an effective ministry, a minimum of six months' salary will provide for the family's catastrophic change in life-style. The church that deals selfishly with its pastor or lets anger blind it to the benefits received during his ministry, causing it to cut him off without a cent, is only hurting itself. It will incur not only the wrath of God but also the resentment of those in the church who loved the pastor. A church's generosity will serve as a testimony to its compassion and will help to cement the pastor's loyal followers to the church. This is no time to be penny wise and pound foolish.

4. URGE THE MINISTER TO LEAVE TOWN IMMEDIATELY

The best service a fallen leader can render his church is to leave as soon as possible so the press cannot interview him. This usually takes one to three months. The less he admits publicly, the less coverage the matter will be given. If possible, he should think of moving his family to another city permanently so he can begin to pick up the pieces of his life. For this reason the church should give him several months of salary, allowing the family to make a new life for itself and permitting him to look for another type of employment. It will also make restoration easier, if that eventually is the way the Lord leads.

Admittedly, severance from church and community will place a severe burden on his entire family, for they must leave friends, school, loved ones, and even extended family members. But after the harm he has inflicted on his church, the best procedure now is to reduce public discussion by leaving the area. As long as he remains in that community, the media may recount his misfortune at every pretext.

The pastor's leaving also will place a burden on the church. It will need to function without its leader. But if he leaves, it may escape the turmoil that often follows the announcement of pastoral infidelity.

5. PREPARE FOR THE MEDIA

Part of the damage control a church will need to face immediately relates to the media. It is safe to say that most members of the media today are no friends of the faith. They thrive on making Christians look foolish, and whenever given the opportunity to discredit the church for the sins of the few, they seize upon it. Once they get a scandalous story about Christians, they play it over and over, like a broken record.

Whether the fallen pastor's church is large or small, its leaders should appoint one person to be the media spokesperson. Ideally, it should be someone with experience in dealing with reporters. Bad news travels fast, appearing as subtle hints or innuendo in the press. If the media manage to leak the information or if you are confident they will cover the pastor's resignation service, *do not stonewall them*. That may cause them to blow the situation well out of proportion. A sizable congregation that expects press coverage should prepare a publicity statement, acknowledging the simplest facts of the pastor's resignation. Be sure to state that the pastor made a full disclosure to the responsible body of the church that accepted his resignation, even admitting the reason for the resignation as moral indiscretion. Include the name of the spokesperson, who should be prepared to return phone calls and answer questions without disclosing more details than will be made public on the Sunday of resignation.

Many media representatives will reward your cooperation and acknowledgment of the sin with a simple report of the event. If you can prevent a full investigation—names, dates, places, etc.—the episode will soon be page 27 news or will be forgotten altogether. If the pastor remains in the area and unwisely starts a new church, you can be sure his past will be dredged up repeatedly.

6. HIRE AN INTERIM MINISTER

Church life must go on! The church will never rest from preaching the Gospel and helping people—and next Sunday is coming. Unless the church has adequate preaching members on the pastoral staff, it will want to find an interim pastor—an experienced, gifted, and sensitive minister, one who will not be a candidate for the permanent position. In this way the church can proceed slowly and prayerfully to seek God's guidance in the selection of a new pastor.

7. ESTABLISH GUIDELINES FOR LEADERSHIP

Most churches have constitutionally established guidelines that pinpoint who is in charge in the absence of the pastor—the chairman of the deacon board, the elder board, the moderator of the church. However, such a person may not be accustomed to taking the helm if the pastor was an active leader. It is very important to establish this person's authority in the eyes of the people.

In every church, power-hungry people will move in to fill any leadership vacuum, whether or not they have the authority. If the pastor was an incisive leader, he may have alienated some of these people because he ran the church without their permission. In his sudden absence, such people come out of the woodwork and can wreak havoc on an already wounded congregation.

One church discovered that its pastor had been disregarding certain elements of the church constitution for some time. Because the pastor was so powerful and popular, no one called him to account—while he was there. But as soon as he resigned, their discontent surfaced, and several members set out to take over the church.

People naturally point fingers of blame when things get out of control, and they commonly turn against the constituted leadership, implying that if they had done their job, this never would have happened. While their evaluation may be faulty, their actions make it difficult for the rightful leaders to assume control unless they act quickly and in unity.

One young church whose pastor resigned immediately appointed the five men who had served as chairmen of the deacon board as the special leadership committee, requesting that they act as final decision makers. That is particularly necessary for a church with a large, full-time staff. The pastor recognized as the leader has departed, and unless an associate minister automatically takes charge, someone must make decisions for the staff and church. One church appointed the executive committee of the board of elders; another chose the officers of the deacon board. Still another appointed a five-man committee, including two of the senior pastors and three board chairmen. It really doesn't matter who composes that committee, but it is important that such a committee be constitutionally designated immediately. This is no time for a conflict between lay leaders and church staff. One church wisely announced a special business meeting for the Sunday night service immediately after the pastor's resignation at the morning service. They then appointed a steering committee. The congregation needs prompt assurance that someone they know is in charge. As a result, those who need answers to their questions have someone to whom they can turn.

At the risk of being repetitious, I must again warn that a minister's resignation for sexual sin is almost invariably followed by enormous hostility within the congregation. Anyone with a gripe about administration, finances, personnel, or program will surface in even the most tranquil congregation when strong leadership has departed. Frustration sweeps through the congregation, and many react in anger. Church officials have been known to threaten one another publicly with bodily harm in the immediate aftermath of the fallen minister's resignation.

At this point the church staff needs reassurance that the local ministry will continue until God sends a new pastor. The church will need to try to keep the membership loss to a minimum, which is usually 10–20 percent. However, one church called an interim pastor who was such a remarkable preacher that, together with the extremely capable staff, he was able to achieve a growth of 10 percent without a pastor. Admittedly, that is rare.

8. ESTABLISH A RESTORATION COMMITTEE

Unless the church's denomination has a procedure for dealing with a fallen pastor, the church should appoint a restoration committee to work with him. To guide this restoration process, the church should designate a small group of three to five people who are spiritually mature, who have maintained a positive relationship with the pastor, and who are well respected by the congregation. Such a committee need not be limited to the elders, though they should have some representation. It could include mature Bible teachers or other board members who have the confidence of the entire church.

The goal of this committee should be to help rebuild the pastor's life—his spiritual life, his marriage, his family life, his relationship to the church body, and his ministry. This rebuilding is a process, one that will take time. The end result of this process may be the pastor's restoration to public ministry. But restoration to ministry is by no means the place to start. The first step is helping the pastor rebuild his spiritual life.

If the pastor and his family have left town permanently, this committee should in Christian love try to keep in touch with them to see that they are getting spiritual help from a sister congregation in their new community. The church mentioned in chapter 11 worked with a fallen pastor who lived in another city through written monthly reports and scheduled visits.

If the pastor has chosen to return to the area after his immediate departure period (as mentioned in #4 above), he should be urged to quietly attend another church in the city but maintain an accountability relationship to this committee commissioned to help him and his family. Not all of the Christian leaders polled in chapter 9 think it wise that the fallen pastor should leave town permanently. Sometimes leaving married children and grandchildren is too traumatic for the wife. Some leaders suggested there is benefit to the body of Christ when a church acts justly in removing the errant pastor but then acts lovingly in helping to rehabilitate his spiritual life, marriage, and family. Then if, at a later date he shows signs of spiritual maturity, they may decide to recommend to the church that he be restored to the ministry.

I feel so strongly about the importance of this committee's functioning that I have devoted an entire chapter to describing the specific responsibilities this committee should carry out in the rebuilding of a fallen pastor's life (see chapter 11).

Above all, the group should not exhibit a vindictive spirit toward the former pastor. One church appointed four men, two staff persons and two officials. The two staff men used their new power to interrogate the broken man in retaliation for what they considered harsh discipline of them when he was in charge. One of the laymen turned on the pastor in bitterness and used his position to inflict further injury on a man who deserved better from people he had otherwise served well for many years. What should have been a restoration committee turned into an inquisition committee, compounding the church's dilemma.

The church is on trial today. The eyes of the world are focused on us, especially when a spiritual leader is involved in sexual immorality. Knowing this, we should take great care to handle these situations so well that outsiders will look at us and say, "See how they loved each other."

9. CUT THE FAT

A pastor's immorality and subsequent resignation can significantly affect a church's finances. This is no time to play financial roulette and expect the church income to continue at the same level it did before the pastor's resignation. A wise church immediately commissions the finance committee to proceed with budget-cutting plans. Usually there is sufficient fat in the budget to handle the expected shortfall.

Begin by eliminating those ministries that were almost totally dependent on the former pastor. Perhaps a TV or radio ministry was subsidized by the church; if the ministry didn't pay its own way before the fall, you can be sure it won't afterward. Even certain staff positions, especially those that were responsible only to the pastor, may be able to be cut.

One large church that suffered such a loss cut a million dollars from its budget within the first month. At this writing they still have not called a pastor, and while the attendance is down almost 20 percent, they are less than .5 percent behind in their budget. That is extraordinary! They are proceeding with an aggressive ministry, primarily because they have retained their most effective staff members. When they finally call a new pastor—and they probably will have done so by the time this book is published—I predict that within one year they will rebuild their attendance and go on ministering in an ever-increasing way.

10. ELECT A SEARCH OR PULPIT COMMITTEE

Everyone needs light at the end of the tunnel, including a congregation. That light clicks on for them as soon as a pulpit search committee is elected, particularly if the people have a voice in its selection. Many churches include this in their constitution, whereas others establish guidelines as the situation arises. One church very carefully sought representation from every group in the church. Starting with the college group, they nominated three representatives from every major department and age group. All were approved by the staff members, and then the church elected one from each group. As it turned out, the committee represented the entire church. It elected its own chairperson, urged the congregation to pray, and kept it apprised of progress, without divulging any names under consideration.

The committee then asked for input from the congregation and received one hundred recommendations. After evaluating the recommendations, the committee reduced the number to forty, and after screening these, they reduced the number to twenty-five people. The committee then reviewed audio/video cassettes of all candidates, without the person's knowledge that he was under consideration. Eventually five top candidates were interviewed until the committee reached a consensus or "the leading of the Spirit." Finally, the committee's prayers were answered, and one man's name became a unanimous choice. He was officially presented to the congregation to preach and meet the people, who then submitted a nearly unanimous call. This time-honored system allows both ample leading of God and the expression of the people.

11. EMPHASIZE FORGIVENESS, LOVE, LOYALTY, AND PRAYER

During the difficult months after the fall of its leader, the congregation needs biblical instruction in four major areas. *Forgiveness* will enable the angry, frustrated, and disillusioned to overcome their reaction to the former leader's sin. In sermons and other teaching times, stress the need and responsibility for *love*—for our Lord, his church, each other, and the pastor's family. Emphasize the need for *loyalty* to the church. This is not the time to abandon ship. Those who have prayed, served, and invested in this church need to support it now more than ever, and they should be urged to give a new pastor at least one year to restore confidence in the ministry of their church. The entire congregation should be urged to *pray*—in groups, in family units, and individually. The church is most vulnerable when it doesn't have a shepherd, but prayer builds a hedge around it.

12. PRACTICE PATIENCE

God is never in a hurry. He wants us to use pressures in our lives to draw us closer to him. If a congregation has been used to leaning heavily on a strong leader, they may have been trusting him instead of the Lord. This chastening experience will return their dependent spirit to the one who deserves it—and that takes time. Many churches are actually better off spiritually for having waited on the Lord to guide them to a suitable successor. They have gained a strengthened heart and have developed greater faith for future ministry.

13. KEEP ON WITH MINISTRY

My uncle, Dr. E. W. Palmer, a pastor for fifty-five years, was one of my heroes in ministry. He once advised me, "Son, always keep a project before your people. Otherwise, you will become their project." That is so true. If the pastorless church submits to the false premise that it should delay any new programs until a pastor is called, they may start to fight and devour one another. They need to lift their sights toward fulfilling the Great Commission and ministering to their community, where troubled people with marriage or family difficulties can't wait for the calling of a new pastor. Unsaved or rebellious Christians may move away before the man of God's choosing comes to lead them. This is an ideal time to enlist many of those who never get involved to participate in door-to-door evangelism, teach classes, or in other ways find their place to serve the Lord.

Many churches will wonder whether or not to continue with some of the special projects that either are being implemented at the time the pastor resigns or are scheduled to start after he will leave. If at all possible, don't cancel such projects. The interim leaders should redouble their prayers and efforts to let God continue to use them in their ministry to others. They might even consider some extra meetings just to encourage the congregation spiritually. While pastoring in San Diego, I received a call from a godly businessman who asked me to come to Michigan to minister for one week in each of two churches, both without pastors. They even flew my wife to minister with me. He made it clear that I wasn't a candidate for the pulpit but was needed as a spiritual shot in the arm to those congregations until the man of God's choosing was called. I was impressed with that kind of thinking, and I eagerly consented.

Churches aren't dependent on leaders. Sometimes we ministers think we are indispensable, forgetting that only God is indispensable! Remember, when God couldn't get a prophet to speak for him, he used a mule. Even without a pastor, any church is better than a mule—if it is willing to be used.

CHAPTER 7

What the Bible Says About Restoration

No single Scripture passage either clearly forbids or clearly approves of restoring a fallen minister to public ministry. For that reason a divergence of opinion on the subject has arisen among Bible-believing Christian leaders, even some who are in basic agreement on most other scriptural issues.

One group has built a negative case with selected passages, insisting that a minister who betrays the sacred trust conferred by God and a loving congregation has lost the right ever to preach again.

A second group, contending that no specific prohibition appears in Scripture, responds that there are no unpardonable sins with God. They believe the Scriptures teach that God is the God of the second chance. Most of the characters in the Bible fell into some form of sin, yet he forgave them and went on to use them mightily.

A third group believes that certain "falls" warrant an extended recovery period. They suggest that every fall should be considered individually to determine whether the leader should be restored to a similar ministry. Several factors should be considered: frequency of the sin, duration of the affair, the number of people involved, and whether the pastor repented before he was caught.

Even denominations don't always agree on this issue. Those who lean toward legalism tend to conclude that a pastor's ministry is forever terminated if he is publicly exposed for adultery. Those whose tradition stresses mercy and grace tend to approve restoration after genuine repentance and an appropriate period of discipline.

Before taking a position, prayerfully consider the following Scripture passages that give guidance about whether or not to restore a fallen pastor to ministry.

WHAT PROVERBS SAYS ABOUT ADULTERY

God hates adultery so much that he made it a capital offense in the Old Testament, as we have already noted. In Proverbs, the book of godly wisdom, he has much to say about the consequences of adultery. Consider the following:

> For the prostitute reduces you to a loaf of bread, and the adulteress preys upon your very life. Can a man scoop fire into his lap without his clothes being burned? Can a man walk on hot coals without his feet being scorched? So is he who sleeps with another man's wife; no one who touches her will go unpunished (Prov. 6:26–29).

> But a man who commits adultery lacks judgment; whoever does so destroys himself. Blows and disgrace are his lot, and his shame will never be wiped away (Prov. 6:32–33).

> With persuasive words she led him astray; she seduced him with her smooth talk. All at once he followed her like an ox going to the slaughter, like a deer stepping into a noose till an arrow pierces his liver, like a bird darting into a snare, little knowing it will cost him his life. Now then, my sons, listen to me; pay attention to what I say. Do not let your heart turn to her ways or stray into her paths. Many are the victims she has brought down; her slain are a mighty throng. Her house

is a highway to the grave, leading down to the chambers
of death (Prov. 7:21–27).

While the target of the passage is prostitutes and what
happens to the man who sleeps with one (which rarely is the
case with fallen pastors), Solomon goes on to discuss
adultery with another man's wife. He then lists the consequences:

- He will not go unpunished.

- He lacks judgment.

- He destroys himself.

- Blows and disgrace are his lot.

- His shame will never be wiped away.

There is no escaping the fact that the act of adultery
carries with it enormous consequences, and they are all bad.
We saw earlier that fallen ministers and their families pay an
awesome price for that sin, even if they are eventually
restored to public ministry.

While some would interpret he "destroys himself" as an
indication that a leader can't ever be restored to ministry, I
would point out that David, the father of the author of
Proverbs, committed adultery with Solomon's mother while
she was married to another man. Yet David continued as
king, and Solomon's mother was permitted to give birth to
the next king who was in the lineage of the Messiah.

SCRIPTURAL QUALIFICATIONS FOR PASTORS

In the New Testament, the apostle Paul enumerates the
qualifications that should be met by any person who would
become a pastor.

> Paul and Timothy, servants of Christ Jesus, To all the
> saints in Christ Jesus at Philippi, together with the
> overseers [bishops] and deacons. This is my prayer: . . .
> that you may be able to discern what is best and may be
> pure and blameless until the day of Christ. Whatever

happens, conduct yourselves in a manner worthy of the gospel of Christ. Do everything without complaining or arguing so that you may become blameless and pure, children of God without fault in a crooked and depraved generation (Phil. 1:1, 9a, 10, 27a; 2:14–15a).

Similarly, encourage the young men to be self-controlled. In everything set them an example by doing what is good. In your teaching show integrity, seriousness and soundness of speech that cannot be condemned, so that those who oppose you may be ashamed because they have nothing bad to say about us. . . . For the grace of God that brings salvation has appeared to all men. It teaches us to say "No" to ungodliness and worldly passions, and to live self-controlled, upright and godly lives in this present age (Titus 2:6–8, 11–12).

Here is a trustworthy saying: If anyone sets his heart on being an overseer, he desires a noble task. Now the overseer must be above reproach, the husband of but one wife, temperate, self-controlled, respectable, hospitable, able to teach, not given to drunkenness, not violent but gentle, not quarrelsome, not a lover of money. He must manage his own family well and see that his children obey him with proper respect. (If anyone does not know how to manage his own family, how can he take care of God's church?) He must not be a recent convert, or he may become conceited and fall under the same judgment as the devil. He must also have a good reputation with outsiders, so that he will not fall into disgrace and into the devil's trap (1 Tim. 3:1–7).

From the above Scripture passages, we can list the following qualifications for a pastor:

- He must be above reproach.
- He must be the husband of one wife.
- He must be temperate.
- He must be self-controlled.
- He must be respectable.
- He must have a good reputation with outsiders.
- He must be a good example.

- He must have integrity.

- He must be able to say no to ungodliness and worldly passion.

God's ideal for pastors is established in these New Testament passages. If a pastor falls short of this standard, loses his church, is publicly humiliated, genuinely repents, receives the forgiveness of God, rebuilds his spiritual life and testimony, and once again confirms his stability, may he be reapproved for public ministry?

Those who believe a pastor can be restored to such ministry point to Paul's public rebuke of the apostle Peter for reverting to legalism, a confrontation which didn't interrupt Peter's ministry (Gal. 2:11–14). But other people will object, "If Peter had committed a moral sin, he might have been disqualified." Others would counter, "He was obviously not above reproach, for Paul said, 'I opposed him to his face because he was clearly in the wrong'" (Gal. 2:11b).

Actually, what Christian leader could say he was always above reproach during his entire ministry? He may not have committed adultery, but what about other sins? Pride, for example, is one of the seven sins God hates. I have known of men who became puffed up with pride until God humbled them through adversity. During their pride-filled days they were not above reproach. Should that period disqualify them from continuing the ministry? If our Lord were to say to every minister who forbids restoration to a fallen colleague after due discipline, "He that is without sin cast the first stone," who would be left to oppose it?

RESTORATION IN SCRIPTURE

What does the Scripture say about restoration? It doesn't give a definitive position, but we can gain some insight from two passages.

Brothers, if someone is caught in a sin, you who are spiritual should restore him gently. But watch yourself, or you also may be tempted. Carry each other's burdens, and in this way you will fulfill the law of Christ (Gal. 6:1–2).

Obviously, the New Testament church believed in restoration for "brothers." It doesn't say whether that includes ministers. On the other hand, there is no reason to believe it does not. Our Lord certainly restored Peter to ministry after he denied him three times. And a good case could be made that denying the Lord three times and with an oath is even worse than adultery!

For God's gifts and his call are irrevocable (Rom. 11:29).

While this verse comes in the midst of a heavy, doctrinal passage about God's call to Israel, who can say it is not one of God's principles that can stand alone? A number of fallen ministers have taken that principle as a challenge to return to ministry in due time and have served the Lord effectively for many years.

A Suggestion

The Scripture passages discussed in this chapter are the major passages used to substantiate the two points of view— for or against restoration to ministry. The next chapter adds insight by examining the lives of several biblical characters who were given a second chance after they had sinned. Study over these two chapters carefully before you read chapters 9 and 10, which describe the positions of several Christian leaders as well as my own. In the final analysis, you will have to study the Scripture, pray, and make your own decision.

CHAPTER 8

Bible Characters to Whom God Gave a Second Chance

These things happened to them as examples and were written down as warnings for us, on whom the fulfillment of the ages has come.

(1 Cor. 10:11)

*T*he more I study human nature, both contemporary and biblical, the more I wonder why God decided to use us in the important work of communicating his Gospel to all mankind. Somehow I think angels would have been more faithful and obedient to his commands. On second thought, Lucifer, the supreme angel, challenged the divine order and forfeited eternal bliss by organizing the first rebellion.

I should not be overly disillusioned with contemporary human nature when I find the Bible filled with illustrations of human frailty. Almost all of the people God used in the Old Testament had feet of clay—particularly where morals were concerned. One salient lesson we can learn from them: the holy God to whom we are reconciled is "a gracious and compassionate God, slow to anger and abounding in love, a God who relents from sending calamity" (Jonah 4:2).

THE GOD OF THE SECOND CHANCE

In teaching children the alphabet, the New England primer proclaims, "In Adam's fall, we sinned all." While Adam was not guilty of adultery, he is a prime example of one of God's errant servants who failed at the assignment he was given. He was commanded *not* to eat of the forbidden fruit, but he did anyway—deliberately.

While he lived in the Garden of Eden, Adam was given the ultimate assignment—to populate the earth. Yet he rebelled against the known will of God and was subsequently expelled from the ideal paradise. God could have gotten rid of Adam and Eve and fashioned a whole new race of perfect people. Instead, he stayed with Adam and Eve and gave them a second chance. God used the sinful couple to fulfill his will. Even their son Cain, the murderer, was offered a second chance to serve God—which he forfeited by further rebellion.

As I read through the Bible, I discover that God used far more people who committed major sins than those who obeyed him implicitly. Quite obviously, disobedience is so pervasive that God found only a few righteous people to carry out his plan.

THE RIGHTEOUS SHORT LIST

Have you ever made a list of God's truly righteous servants mentioned in the Bible? The most exemplary seems to be Enoch, the pre-flood prophet who lived to be 365 years old. He was so in tune with God that he was one of only two people in the Bible who were taken directly into God's presence without physically dying. Although we are not told many details about Enoch's life, we are told the most important one: he "walked with God."

Then there is Noah, the faithful prophet who built the ark and preached to the godless people of his generation for 120 years. This preacher of righteousness (2 Pet. 2:5) was described in (Gen. 6:9) as "a righteous man, blameless among the people of his time, and he walked with God."

The final chapters of Genesis are devoted to the adventures of a remarkable young man who reflected as much moral fortitude and dynamic leadership as anyone else in the Old Testament. Joseph, the son of Jacob and Rachel, endured the vicissitudes of life both at home and in Egypt, without forsaking God or lowering his standard of faith and righteousness. Beginning with his youthful dream, which incurred the wrath of his brothers, Joseph was subjected to filial rejection, servitude in Egypt, the temptation and lies of Potiphar's wife, the unjust anger of his master, and the thoughtlessness of a chief cupbearer. Through patience and the exercise of his gift of dream interpretation, he rose to power in Pharaoh's kingdom and guided the nation through a period of famine. At the peak of his success, when he could have returned evil for evil, he exercised a forgiving attitude and a gracious spirit of love toward his family. Joseph endured bravely, used his God-given talents wisely, and transformed family animosity into a bond of love. Although he had more than one wife, he fell neither to the wiles of evil women nor to the natural desire for revenge. The Bible holds up Joseph as a model of faith and faithfulness.

Samuel, the prophet, priest, and judge, is another godly servant against whom there is no negative comment. He led Israel in one of its darkest days as judge until the people demanded a king. He then anointed the first two kings, Saul and David, and turned the nation over to them. He faithfully served God during his entire life.

Then comes Daniel, a godly, spiritually sensitive, and morally upright young man. Beset with cultural pressure, the antagonism of his peers, pagan rulers, and fierce lions, he faced his difficulties with spiritual strength and divine wisdom. However, it must be pointed out that the exemplary Daniel was made a eunuch in his teens, so sexual temptation was nonexistent for him.

Although we could list other morally pure Old Testament servants—prophets like Elijah, Elisha, Jeremiah, and Isaiah; kings like Josiah—the list is short.

THE UNRIGHTEOUS LONG LIST

Of the hundreds of people God used in history, the overwhelming majority were fallen servants—not only as children of Adam and Eve but also in the exercise of their own free will. They chose to sin—quite grievously. Yet in most cases, God did not remove his hand from their lives. True, they paid a terrible price in personal suffering for their sin, a penalty that extended to their family and friends, but the God of the second chance did use them *after* their failures.

Abraham, the Adulterer

The New Testament gives more space to Abraham than to any other Old Testament figure, an indication that Abraham found unusual favor with God. He overcame his fear and developed into such a remarkable model of faith that the New Testament refers to him as the man who "believed God, and it was credited to him as righteousness" (Rom. 4:3).

Yet Abraham committed adultery with his wife's servant, Hagar (Gen. 16:2–4). The fact that Abraham was told by his wife to take Hagar as a mistress, supposedly to fulfill God's will, does not absolve him of adultery. Abraham knew better, yet he did not argue with Sarah when she urged him to sleep with Hagar. In the wake of a sinful choice came extensive suffering to both Abraham and Sarah as well as Hagar, Ishmael, and millions of people ever since. The world today would be vastly different if Abraham had never committed adultery with Hagar and fathered the Arab race. Yet God used him to fulfill his will—to father the Hebrew nation—*after* his adultery.

Moses, the Murderer

Moses was truly one of the great men in the Bible. God used Moses not only to lead the children of Israel out of Egypt toward the Promised Land but also to deliver the Ten Commandments, his moral law.

But Moses had a problem with his anger. Once when he saw an Egyptian fighting with an Israelite, he killed the Egyptian. Then later on in his life after receiving the Ten Commandments, he came down the mountain and saw the gross immorality of the people. In a rage, he threw down the stone tablets on which the Lord had written his moral law, breaking the tablets into pieces.

However, Moses became a prominent leader in God's program for Israel *after* he murdered the Egyptian. Both Israel and the entire Christian church are grateful that God gave Moses a second chance.

But God does have a limit to which he indulges our sin. After many expressions of anger, Moses blew up one time too many. He struck the rock in a fit of rage when God had told him to speak to the rock. For this disobedience, Moses was not allowed to enter the Promised Land. A possible lesson we can learn from his life, as well as the lives of Saul, Samson, and the others, is that in the Old Testament at least, men did not lose their divine calling for simple acts of sin, but for many acts of sin over a long period of time, showing they were in basic rebellion to the will of God.

Samson, the Fornicator

Every Sunday-school graduate remembers the story of Samson, the special servant of God who was endowed with supernatural strength. Samson was a mighty man of war against the enemies of Israel, killing a thousand Philistines at one time. Yet he dissipated his great gift with self-indulgence. Early in his life he boasted, wagered, then killed thirty men just to get their clothes for payment of a bet he had lost. His sensuality led him to lust, immorality, and finally to breaking his Nazirite vow by drinking wine and having his hair cut. When he violated his covenant with God, God no longer gave him strength.

Samson paid dearly for his sin. He was blinded by the Philistines and forced to grind in the prison house of his enemies. Yet the God of the second chance once more endowed Samson with special power in response to his prayer. At the peak of a pagan religious festival, God enabled him to kill more people in his death than he did in his life.

Samson's tragic story seems to picture today's fallen leader, whose judgment, in proportion to his sin, seriously limits God's use of his life. After sufficient repentance and rebuilding, he may regain favor in God's eyes, but he is never able to reach the heights for which he seemed destined, if he had walked in moral obedience to his Master.

David, the King-sized Sinner

David, one of the most admired Old Testament men, was called "the man after God's own heart." His psalms have been a source of rich spiritual blessing to millions of Christians as they experience trial and testing. Yet the enormity of David's sin, in the light of circumstances, makes him one of the grossest moral sinners among leaders in the Bible. Although God was very real to David, he was vulnerable to sexual sin.

The pattern of David's sin, which Bible scholars project over some eighteen months of his life, forms the prototype for progressive sin—a Christian leader advancing from a small sin to a larger one until he can even commit adultery. The Scripture describes the situation, perhaps a time of mid-life crisis, when wearing the crown had become routine.

In the spring, at the time when kings go off to war, David sent Joab out with the king's men and the whole Israelite army. They destroyed the Ammonites and besieged Rabbah. But David remained in Jerusalem. One evening David got up from his bed and walked around on the roof of the palace. From the roof he saw a woman bathing. The woman was very beautiful, and David sent someone to find out about her. The man said, "Isn't this Bathsheba, the daughter of Eliam and the wife of Uriah the Hittite?" Then David sent messengers to get her. She came to him, and he slept with her (2 Sam. 11:1–4a).

Instead of leading the people into battle, David became complacent with pride, sent his subordinates to fulfill his military duties, and consequently was tempted by lust that he would never have faced had he been doing God's will. Lasciviousness and greed led him to consider himself above the rules God had established for all married men, and he took possession of another man's wife. That was followed by desperate attempts to cover his sin, which included lying, betrayal, and even murder.

David is a classic example of one who harbors a character flaw that is just waiting to be unleashed. One improper military choice led to lust, and when it was conceived, it brought forth sin (see James 1:15).

A close look at David's life after that sin provides ample evidence that "the way of transgressors is hard" (Prov. 13:15 KJV). The great tragedies of David's life followed his sin. David and his entire family paid dearly for his sin of immorality. David was known as a fallen leader the rest of his life. According to Nathan the prophet, "Because by doing this you have made the enemies of the Lord show utter contempt [or "blaspheme"], the son born to you will die" (2 Sam. 12:14).

But David's life *after* his sin also serves as an example that although God will judge his servant, he does not carry a grudge. Some of the most productive ministry of David's life followed his sin and repentance. After this event he consolidated the great kingdom of Israel and ruled for almost thirty years. He planned the great temple and gathered the materials to build it. After his fall David also wrote most of the great psalms that have given solace to millions of God's people in times of despair. And it was during his period of restoration that he fathered and raised the next king of Israel. Perhaps most amazing of all is the fact that the woman he committed adultery with became the mother of Solomon, the next king. The extent of God's forgiveness is inestimable.

Jonah, the Rebellious and Disobedient Prophet

The biblical record mentions no immorality in Jonah's personal life. But he certainly is notorious for his rebellion against the known will of God. After God had explicitly told Jonah to go to Nineveh, he sailed in the opposite direction. Such overt disobedience was inexcusable.

God wanted to bless the Ninevites with godly repentance and produce a moral-spiritual revival that would transform an entire culture, but Jonah refused to be a part of it. He was a nationalistic bigot. He hated the Ninevites for all the suffering they had inflicted on the children of Israel through the centuries. He obviously didn't want them to repent and escape the doom of God's judgment.

When Jonah's undisguised rebellion caused him to board a ship for the opposite direction, God sent a storm (judgment). The sailors threw him into the sea, and he was swallowed by a great fish. After three days and three nights of prayer and contrition, Jonah was regurgitated up onto dry land. Finally Jonah obeyed God's original instructions, preaching judgment and repentance to the Ninevites.

The now-submissive preacher experienced the greatest revival recorded in human history. Scripture tells us that God granted this revival because Nineveh had "more than a hundred and twenty thousand people who cannot tell their right hand from their left" (Jonah 4:11). Some commentators indicate that this number refers to small children, suggesting that perhaps as many as one million Ninevites repented and turned to God. What contemporary preacher wouldn't like that kind of results from an entire lifetime of ministry, even with television and radio? Yet as the narrative concluded, Jonah was still displeased because he had wanted these people to pay for their persecution of his nation.

The God of the second chance used Jonah in an incredible way *after* his defiance and deliberate rebellion in the face of explicit instructions. Only eternity will reveal what could have been accomplished with his life as a "city-wide evangelist" if he had been a totally obedient prophet.

Peter, the Betrayer

A deeply disillusioned Christian leader, upon hearing the sad news of the fall of a friend of mine, exclaimed, "I don't believe God will ever use him again as a preacher of the Word!"

I found the woman's outburst so dogmatic that I challenged her, "Which sin is worse: adultery or a direct denial of the Lord?"

She responded warily, "Well, I suppose denial of the Lord." I pointed out that the apostle Peter publicly denied his relationship to Jesus three times! Yet *after* this denial, God used him to preach the Gospel to both the Jews and the Gentiles. He went on to become the leader of the early church for approximately the first fifteen years of the spread of Christianity. The God of the second chance accepted Peter's genuine repentance and restored him to ministry.

The apostle John recorded the Lord's restoration of Peter following the Resurrection—*after* Peter had repented and wept bitterly. Jesus recommissioned Peter by charging him three times to "feed my sheep"—one directive for each denial.

These are only some of the fallen people God used. The Bible records many others. Our God—the God of the second chance—mercifully forgives repentant sinners and uses them even *after* they have fallen.

CHAPTER 9

What Some Christian Leaders Say About Restoration

Dr. Russ Dilday, my friend and winter ski partner, is also president of the largest seminary in the world, Southwestern Baptist Seminary in Fort Worth, Texas. On a ski lift shortly after the public confession of Jimmy Swaggart, we were discussing the well-laid out policy of the Assemblies of God denomination for restoring its fallen leaders. "Russ," I asked, "if that happened to a Southern Baptist leader (and it has), what policy would we have for dealing with such a problem?"

He responded, "We don't have one! Every church responds to that issue autonomously."

No wonder one of the most dynamic pastors in the Southeast has divorced his wife and married his secretary, yet at this writing he is still the pastor of the congregation where it all took place. Instead of disciplining him and demanding his resignation, his deacons have forgiven him and have stood behind his decision to remain as their pastor. Because the denomination itself has no set policy for dealing with such situations, they are virtually powerless to intervene.

Several independent Baptist churches have fared no

better. During the months I have been writing this book, the scandalous sexual behavior of the pastor of one of the country's largest churches has come to light. The story has appeared in several Christian journals, exposing an immoral life-style that goes back at least eighteen years. Although attendance at his church has declined drastically and his budget had to be cut severely as a result of the publication of accusations alleged to be from one of his secretaries (the wife of one of his deacons), he has denied it all, refusing to step down or submit to an impartial investigation by his peers. There is apparently nothing anyone can do to rid his church of him.

Most Baptist and independent churches would not put up with such scandals. Upon finding sufficient evidence, they would call a meeting of the church leaders and fire the man. However, when confronted with a powerful pastor who refuses to cooperate, they seem almost paralyzed.

Such behavior is not limited to one ideology. I know of both liberals and fundamentalists who have committed gross sin, sidestepped the allegations, ridden out the storm, and continued to preach. One such fundamentalist pastor has probably held more "pastors' conferences on soul winning" than any other man in the country, and once he bragged that if anything happened to him, it would "destroy the fundamentalist movement." An ego like that is vulnerable to moral indiscretion because, as we noted previously, such a man considers himself above the rules—even the edicts of God.

However, such powerfully strong-willed men are rare. Churches normally can muster enough leadership among their lay leaders to oust the offender and restore moral order. But doing the "right thing" when a fallen pastor will not step aside or submit to an impartial investigation is always messy and leaves the church scarred for years to come.

100,000 CHURCHES HAVE NO POLICY

Many denominations have established a set policy for handling such situations. For example, the Assemblies of

God, Nazarenes, Wesleyan Methodists, and Presbyterians hold the credentials of their ministers; consequently they can "defrock" them after thorough investigation and prayerful evaluation. Baptist and independent groups, which include 100,000 churches in the United States, have no such model. Each church holds to "the autonomy of the local church." Unfortunately, this has given license to some rather bizarre behavior through the years. But as leaders are quick to inform us, establishing a hierarchy over the clergy would have worse consequences.

Since so many churches have failed to outline a procedure for public censure of an adulterous minister and since the Scripture is not explicit about this issue, I took a survey among respected ministers throughout the country. If we could find a consensus among these leaders, we could begin to design a possible model that churches could use to confront the problem of ministerial infidelity.

I hope that this chapter and the next few will spark discussion that may soon establish a comprehensive model that is both biblical and fair to the fallen leader and his church—a model that will demonstrate the mercy of God and his church and instill a spirit of responsibility, enabling us to deal properly with this moral problem.

THE QUESTIONNAIRE

I designed the following questionnaire so that busy pastors could respond in a minimum period of time. The original tool comprised eleven questions, including some about ministerial divorce. I have included in this chapter their responses to the first six questions, those dealing with moral failure.

1. Do you believe a pastor, minister, or Christian leader who commits adultery can ever be restored to the gospel ministry?

2. What Scripture passages do you give to support your position?
3. If your answer to Question #1 was "Yes," what minimum conditions should be met before he "goes public"?
4. If your answer to Question #1 was "Yes," how long should he stay out of the public ministry before he returns to the pulpit?
5. In your opinion, should he move to another part of the country before starting a new ministry?
6. If your answer to Question #1 was "Yes," what waiting period would you prescribe for the man who had already dealt with his sin, sincerely repented, and was restored to his wife several months before his sexual sin became public knowledge?

The differences in the men's responses indicate that there is no approved solution. In general, the Assemblies of God men, probably because of denominational policy, believe that restoration to a preaching ministry is possible. Baptists are divided. As you will see, they all require some form of proving period and continual accountability.

The leaders I polled include:

Dr. G. Ray Carlson, general superintendent of the Assemblies of God

Dr. Glen Cole, pastor of Capital Christian Center, Sacramento

Dr. W. A. Criswell, pastor of First Baptist Church, Dallas

Dr. Edward G. Dobson, pastor of Calvary Church, Grand Rapids

Dr. Jimmy Draper, pastor of First Baptist Church, Euless, Texas

Dr. Jerry Falwell, pastor of Thomas Road Baptist Church, Lynchburg, Virginia

Dr. Richard C. Halverson, chaplain of the United States Senate

Dr. Jack Hayford, pastor of The Church On The Way, Van Nuys, California

Dr. David Hocking, pastor of Calvary Church, Santa Ana, California

Dr. John A. Huffman, Jr., pastor of St. Andrew's Presbyterian Church, Newport Beach, California

Dr. Richard Lee, pastor of Rehoboth Baptist Church, Atlanta, Georgia

Dr. John MacArthur, Jr., pastor of Grace Community Church, Sun Valley, California

Dr. Ross Rhoads, pastor of Calvary Church, Charlotte, North Carolina

Dr. Charles Swindoll, pastor of First Evangelical Free Church, Fullerton, California

DR. G. RAY CARLSON AND THE ASSEMBLIES OF GOD MODEL

Since the Assemblies of God denomination offers the most definitive model with which I am familiar, we will consider it first. Dr. G. Ray Carlson, the general superintendent of the denomination, graciously supplied me with the appropriate portion of the Assemblies of God constitution and bylaws. Note in the introductory portion that the waiting period is listed under "disciplinary action." This is a concept that needs to be evaluated by the independent and Baptist-style churches, because the restoration period of a fallen minister is not just a matter of waiting. It is a matter of church discipline that will have a positive effect on the fallen minister's spiritual and moral life, equipping him once again for the ministry. I have reprinted here the most pertinent passages from the bylaws.

ARTICLE IX. DISCIPLINE
A. DISTRICT ACTION

Section 1. The Nature and Purpose of Discipline

Discipline is an exercise of scriptural authority for which the church is responsible. The aims of discipline are that God may be honored, that the purity and welfare of the ministry may be maintained, and that those under discipline may be brought to repentance and restoration.

Discipline is to be administered for the restoration of the minister, while fully providing for the protection of the spiritual welfare of our local assemblies. It is to be redemptive in nature as well as corrective and is to be exercised as under a dispensation of mercy.

Section 2. Causes of Disciplinary Action

Violation of Assemblies of God principles as stated in these Constitution and Bylaws may give cause for disciplinary action by the Credentials Committee. Among such causes for action shall be:

a. Any conduct unbecoming to a minister or indiscretions involving morals. . . .

Section 7. Credentials Terminations

In all cases the minister shall be requested to surrender his Certificate of Ordination and his current fellowship card to the district office. The district shall forward these to the office of the general secretary of The General Council of the Assemblies of God. Refusal to surrender his Certificate of Ordination and current fellowship card shall be considered insubordination and may result in placing a charge against the minister.

Section 9. Rehabilitation

When it has been determined, either by a confession of the minister involved or by deliberation of the district presbytery, that there is a cause for disciplinary action as a result of a violation of Assemblies of God principles as set forth in Article IX, A, Section 2, it shall then be the responsibility of the district presbytery to determine whether or not the offense warrants expulsion from the Fellowship by dismissal or restoration to good standing in the Fellowship through a program of rehabilitation. Recognizing that the underlying principle involved in discipline is redemptive, and that man's conscience frequently brings him to judgment and confession, and that justice can sometimes best be served with mercy; therefore, the following provisions for rehabilitation shall apply:

a. Basis. Those found to have violated any of the Assemblies of God principles (Article IX, A, Section 2) shall be subject to a period of rehabilitation.

b. Period of time. The period of rehabilitation shall be not less than 1 year except when the violation involves misconduct defined in Article IX, A, Section 2, paragraph a, in which case it shall be for not less than 2 years.

c. Procedure and requirements. The following procedure shall be used by the district presbytery in determining the specific requirements of rehabilitation for the individual minister.

1.) *Suspension.* The minister shall be considered to be under suspension during the entire period of rehabilitation, and his credentials shall be held in the district office. The extent to which he may be permitted to minister, if any, shall be determined by the district presbytery. Certain offenses may not require complete cessation of ministerial activities, although some restrictions or limitations may be warranted.

2.) *District member with conditions.* The minister must remain a member of the district during the period of rehabilitation. While his credentials are in a state of suspension, his name shall not be published as removed from the ministerial roster. In the event his ministerial activity has been terminated, the minister must become established in a local church working under the supervision of a pastor and presbyter.

3.) *District progress reports.* The Credentials Committee of the district shall submit to the Credentials Committee of the General Council on February 1 and August 1 of each calendar year a progress report relative to the rehabilitation of ministers under discipline.

4.) *Minister's reports.* The minister must submit reports quarterly to the district superintendent.

5.) *Classified information.* The rehabilitation record shall not accompany the Certificate of Transfer to another district. The information shall be preserved for future reference in the files of the district and the Credentials Committee of the General Council of the Assemblies of God.

6.) *Completion of rehabilitation.* When the rehabilitation period is satisfactorily completed, the minister shall be considered in good standing and his credentials restored.[1]

The entire body of Christ owes a debt of gratitude to Dr. Carlson and the other leaders of the Assemblies of God denomination for the excellent manner in which they handled the sexual misconduct of Jimmy Swaggart. Even though the Swaggart ministry had contributed $12 million dollars annually to the Assemblies of God missionary causes, they refused to make an exception for him. They removed his credentials, as they would have done to any other minister for committing similar sins. They then voted to remove him from ministry for one year, requiring that he submit to counseling for two years. Unfortunately, Mr. Swaggart chose to reject their authority and withdrew from the denomination after only three months out of ministry, discrediting himself even further with the Christian community. The denomination acted so responsibly and lovingly that they earned the respect of fair-minded people everywhere in proving that Christians do hold even their most famous leaders accountable.

Because the sexual misconduct of Jim Bakker and Jimmy Swaggart received nationwide media coverage, Dr. Carlson was required to answer many questions from both within and outside his own denomination. Consequently, he developed a form letter that covers many of the issues addressed in my questionnaire. His answers, most of which I have included, show his depth of research.

God's standard of conduct is high and is the same for church leaders and those who are not looked upon as church leaders. However, church leaders have a much greater responsibility due to the fact their influence is greater. Jesus said, "For unto whomsoever much is given, of him shall be much required" (Luke 12:48). "My brethren, be not many masters [literally, "teachers"], knowing that we shall receive the greater condemnation" (James 3:1). Ministers are to be examples of the believers . . . in purity (1 Tim. 4:12), blameless (1 Tim. 3:2), and have a good report of them which are without (1 Tim. 3:7).

It is a serious thing to put a stumbling block or an occasion to fall in a brother's way (Rom. 14:13, 21). If the foregoing conditions are the basis for having a divinely approved ministry, they are also the basis for maintaining and perpetuating such ministry.

Two things need to be set in proper perspective: (1) Discipline has nothing to do with whether a person has been forgiven of his sin by either God or man. It is on the basis of a person's forgiveness that he submits to the disciplinary process. (2) Discipline is not punishment; it is redemptive and restorative. It provides time for a healing process to take place to enable a fallen minister to have the assurance he has overcome his weakness and temptation, and to restore confidence in others that he has been truly rehabilitated.

In Galatians 6:1 those who are spiritual are charged to restore those overtaken in a fault. This again is not referring to the restoration of a ministry, but to the restoration of one found out to have sinned to fellowship with God and the body of believers. The Greek word translated "restore" has the meaning of "to mend," as in the healing of a broken bone. The tense is the continuous present, suggesting the necessity of patience and perseverance in the process.

The example of Peter leading the company of believers and preaching the gospel within 40 days after his denial of Christ with cursing, should not be taken as the standard criterion of how to deal with ministers who sin. Peter's sin was not hypocritical or done in secret, but was an impulsive act out of fear while in a temporary backslidden condition. Despite his boastful assertion of following the Lord even unto death, the Lord warned him aforetime of his denial, but also told him that he had prayed that his faith not fail, and when he was converted he was to strengthen his brethren (Luke 22:31–34). Almost immediately after he sinned, without any prompting, Peter voluntarily repented and went out and wept bitterly (Luke 22:62). This is rare. Most ministers who sin attempt to hide their sin and admit it only when they are caught. Before His ascension, our Lord recommissioned Peter (John 21:15–17).

Our greatest concern in these days of compromise and moral laxity is that sin not be looked upon too lightly. A ministry with high visibility has a much greater responsibility, and this must be taken into account in the administration of discipline. No one can evade his responsibility to the entire body of Christ, for we are members one to another.

DR. GLEN COLE

In 1978, Dr. Glen Cole accepted the call to the Capital Christian Center of Sacramento, California. Dr. Cole has a regular television and radio ministry, serves on the board of many Christian organizations, is the key leader among pastors of that area in efforts to return his community to moral sanity, and was a member of the executive committee of the Assemblies of God Church when it had to deal with the fall of Jim Bakker and Jimmy Swaggart.

Like others in his denomination, Pastor Cole believes that a fallen minister can be restored to the gospel ministry—after a minimum period of two years. He would make an exception for the minister who judged his own sin privately, gained God's forgiveness, and went on to experience God's blessing on his ministry for several years before his sin was exposed. In such a case, he believes a fallen minister could be brought back into ministry after one year, if so "determined by a group of brethren who can analyze the severity of his reaction to the sin." He would not require a fallen minister to move to another part of the country but does feel that a change of churches and immediate location is best for him, his family, and the body of Christ.

During the time this book was being written, one of my minister friends (whose sin had been exposed several years after he had confessed it to God and enjoyed God's blessing on his ministry) began to attend Glen's church. The minister and his wife needed love and pastoring during their waiting period, and they found it at Capital Christian Center. Now that the year-long waiting period is over, Pastor Cole worked with other local pastors in helping to arrange a restoration program for him. A public recommissioning service was conducted, and subsequently he was invited to join the staff of a church as co-pastor. This fortunate congregation will now enjoy the benefits of his many talents and new commitment to living a godly life. This experience could serve as a positive model for Christian leaders seriously interested in restoring fallen ministers, who then can proceed to use their lives, talents, and years of experience to advance the kingdom of God.

DR. W. A. CRISWELL

For over forty years Dr. Criswell has pastored the largest church in the Southern Baptist Convention, the First Baptist Church of Dallas, Texas. At over eighty years of age, he is considered by many people to be the dean of modern pastors. His contributions to Christianity are legendary as an orator, pastor, author, denominational leader, and television and radio minister.

Dr. Criswell believes that the ministry is such a sacred trust that any man who violates his marriage vows is no longer entitled to be a senior pastor. He did not answer the questionnaire but sent the following statement:

> In God's Book we are told that our Lord casts our sins behind His back, that He buries them in the depths of the sea, and that He remembers them against us no more. In that goodness of God, we all rejoice.
>
> But the problem of the minister in the pulpit who has committed adultery or who has sinned grievously in other areas assails me and confronts me as a listener. What do *I* do when I sit there in the audience and look at that man who represents the Lord and know that he has been unfaithful to his vows, both to the Spirit of Holiness that called him into the ministry and to the life of virtue that accompanies his calling. No matter how I tried, I could never get beyond the fact that this man has betrayed his trust. It seems to me, therefore, that for the sake of his listening audience he ought to seek employment in some other area of life. God forgives him, we forgive him, but that does not mean he must continue as a

minister of the gospel. He can serve the Lord who has forgiven him in some other capacity.

DR. EDWARD G. DOBSON

After serving faithfully as a popular college professor at Liberty University and as a Bible teacher in his local church, Dr. Dobson accepted a call to the historic Calvary Church of Grand Rapids, Michigan, where he is enjoying an outstanding ministry. A prolific author, noted for readable scholarship, he has written several books, including one about marriage and divorce.

In response to the questionnaire, Dr. Dobson sent an article he had just written for the *Fundamentalist Journal.* Like most of the others who responded, he bases his belief in restoration on Galatians 6:1. But he identifies four areas in which this restoration should take place.

1. **Restoration to Fellowship:** When ministers default in their personal lives, it is sin. It is not spiritual burnout or mid-life crisis—it is sin against God. David certainly recognized this fact after he had committed adultery with Bathsheba and attempted to cover it up by murdering her husband. A casual reading of his psalm of confession underscores the reality of his sin against God (Psalm 51). Sin requires repentance and confession. Only then can fellowship with God be restored.

2. **Restoration to Worship:** Where does a fallen leader turn for help and support? He should turn to a local church— God's agency for discipline, care, and spiritual growth. After being restored to fellowship with God, the leader needs restoration to an assembly of believers where he and his family can receive love, care, discipline, and accountability. [He then points out that in 2 Corinthians 2:6–8, Paul instructed the church of Corinth to restore to worship the brother whom he had told them to discipline in 1 Corinthians 5.]

3. **Restoration to service:** The third step of restoration is the restoring of service to that person by giving him opportunities to exercise his spiritual gift(s). This does not mean leadership—rather it involves service. To deny such a person service is to deny him the joy of exercising his God-given

spiritual gifts. To deny him service is to abort the overall functioning of the gifts within the body.

4. **Restoration to leadership:** In attempting to resolve the issue of leadership, we must examine the nature and extent of the sin. Some pastors never committed adultery, but they have been emotionally entangled with someone to the point where resignation was necessary. Some pastors fall prey to one encounter. Others have carried on affairs for years with one or more people in their congregation. It appears that a continued life-style of sexual sin over a period of time would disqualify a person from leadership, since his reputation could not be sufficiently restored (1 Tim. 3), whereas those who fall prey to one emotional or physical encounter may be restored. . . . It appears that with discipline, accountability, love, forgiveness, and time, some fallen leaders can be restored to public ministry and leadership. However, I am not the one to make final judgment. I can be involved in restoring them to fellowship, worship, and service. It is up to God to restore them to leadership in His timing and place. I must be hesitant to condemn that restoration lest I be guilty of fighting against God.[2]

Dr. Dobson makes no attempt to identify the waiting period when the fallen minister is out of public ministry. He leaves that to God and the local elders, who must make that decision in light of the person's sin and repentance. Dr. Dobson concludes, "I am concerned that we do not lose our perspective on the overriding theme of Scripture—grace, redemption, and forgiveness. I am [also] concerned that we do not forget that the Scriptures are filled with saints who failed, repented, and were restored to fellowship, service, and leadership."[3]

DR. JIMMY DRAPER

Dr. Jimmy Draper pastors the First Baptist Church of Euless, Texas, a suburb of Dallas. For two years Dr. Draper served as president of the Southern Baptist Convention and is still active in denominational concerns, both in his state and nationally. The author of several books, Dr. Draper is outspoken about his concern for a moral-spiritual revival in our country and culture. The pastors of his denomination consider him "a friend of pastors."

Dr. Draper's response to my survey was both thorough and unique.

The New Testament is largely silent on this issue [of ministerial restoration]. There is no example of a New Testament pastor or minister who committed immorality. However, there are some principles by which we are guided.

First, sin is sin for all believers. There is no distinction. What is distinguished is that God holds the leader to a more strict accountability (James 3:1).

Second, Christian leaders are not pastors, teachers, or evangelists (Eph. 4:11) because they are super-saints. They are such because of the gift of the Holy Spirit. Leadership is not so much an achievement of the leader as it is a grace gift of the Holy Spirit. In the New Testament church there was not the current distinction of "clergy" vs. "laity." All were called to serve (Rom. 1:6) and served out of their spiritual gift and calling.

Thus, the sin should be dealt with on an individual basis. The common denominator is the sin, not the person's position.

"Gospel ministry" takes in a wide range of activities. Are we asking if a pastor commits adultery, can he be restored to the pastorate of a church of similar size? Or are we asking if a pastor commits adultery, can he be restored to some position within the framework of the gospel ministry?

I would be very hesitant to play the Holy Spirit. As one dear friend said, "God can do anything but fail." So, of course, one can be restored.

The classic example of a leader being restored is that of King David. Leviticus 20:10 prescribed the death penalty for any Israelite's adultery. But God pardoned David and restored him to his position of leadership. However, it was not without consequence. The sword never left his house, and although a leader, he lost both loyalty and respect. And David was not publicly exposed! (cf. 2 Sam. 11–12ff as well as Ps. 32 and Ps. 51).

Another example is Samson (Judg. 13:2–16:31). Although a Nazirite, Samson was a life-style womanizer. He was forgiven and used by God in the final act of his life. But God allowed him to fall and never be restored to his position.

The biblical doctrine of the discipline of a believer comes into focus. It appears that God first speaks to us through the Holy Spirit and Scripture. If a person refuses to repent, God may send or allow some type of circumstance that will get that person's attention and turn him to the Lord. In the process of his seeking God about one area, God may seek him in another. But it also appears that public exposure is also a method of divine discipline.

Samson and the man in 1 Corinthians 5 (who was in an incestuous relationship) were publicly exposed. It can be argued that David was not publicly exposed in the sense that all knew what was happening. His treatment of Bathsheba (marriage after the death of her husband) is one evidence of this.

Thus, I conclude that if a leader commits adultery or fornication and responds to the conviction of the Holy Spirit and seeks to be restored, there is great hope for restoration.

But if the leader's moral sin is life-style and the Lord allows public exposure, I tend to believe that man will never rise to the same leadership level. I further believe that man's restoration to leadership can come only after a very lengthy time of counseling and rehabilitation and will be on a much smaller scale.

Dr. Draper offered this analysis for the conditions required before a fallen minister is restored:

It is largely a local church issue. But there should be enough time to allow folks to see that the person has indeed repented and has led a life-style of fruitful repentance.

Just saying "I have sinned, I have repented" is not enough. Of course, God's forgiveness is instantaneous. However, you must keep in mind that adultery is more than a sexual sin. It is also a sin of deceit. You do not rebuild trust overnight.

We must also remember that there are more relationships involved than just vertical. There are numerous horizontal relationships (the man and his spouse, family, church, friends, neighbors, public, etc.). There should be continued accountability.

We must take care not to build an artificial "Restoration Process." By that I mean that we evangelicals are very fond of doing everything by steps: "Seven steps to this," "Four steps to that." If we are not careful, we will build an artificial (and legalistic) process. Each case should be treated on an individual basis. Where Scripture speaks, we must speak. Where Scripture is silent, we must use extreme wisdom.

Dr. Draper made these comments about the length of the waiting period:

Again, this should be on an individual basis. But I would distinguish between the individual who confessed to God and initiated his own restorative process and the individual who was publicly exposed and forced into "repentance."

He may never return to the pulpit. It may be wise for some of these brethren to reenter ministry as associates, accountable to someone else. It is possible to be in ministry without being "King Kong."

The very nature of these questions is part of the problem. We seem to have forgotten that ministry demands a "servant" motif and not a "serve me" motif (cf. John 13). I cannot understand why a *God-called* man would not be thrilled at any second chance to rebuild and to serve God, even if it means he starts back as an associate somewhere. I have little sympathy or respect for a man who won't serve. A demanding spirit is evidence of a non-repentant spirit. That does not mean that one's heart desire cannot be to lead once again. . . . A repentant man will be a servant.

DR. JERRY FALWELL

Jerry Falwell is easily the best-known Baptist preacher in America and perhaps the world. He has pastored in Lynchburg, Virginia, at the Thomas Road Baptist Church, which grew from a handful of people to one of the largest churches in the country. His congregation also includes millions of television viewers who consider him their television pastor. His love for other pastors is reflected in the many conferences he conducts for them and in his goal of "training 5,000 preachers who will start new churches"—and that doesn't include the thousands of young people preparing for the ministry at his Liberty University and Seminary. We would be hard pressed to find any minister in this generation who has done more to help pastors, build the kingdom of God, and try to restore some degree of moral sanity to the American culture.

Dr. Falwell finds in 1 Timothy 3:1–7 sufficient indication that fallen ministers are not entitled to return to a preaching ministry. He does feel, however, that if they have shown adequate signs of repentance, they can be used in another capacity. However, even then it should only be after "complete repentance, full restitution and forgiveness ... followed by an extensive program of accountability and counsel." Once that is accomplished, he feels that a move to another part of the country "might be desirable in terms of family considerations and in rebuilding integrity."

DR. RICHARD C. HALVERSON

While serving as an associate on the staff of the Hollywood Presbyterian Church, where he had a powerful ministry to businessmen, Dr. Halverson was invited to Washington, D. C., to work with the prayer-breakfast ministry. A few years later, he became the senior pastor of the Fourth Presbyterian Church of Bethesda, Maryland, where he has served for the past twenty-three years. One of the hallmarks of his ministry is his deeply spiritual and highly practical teaching of God's Word. During the past nine years Dr. Halverson has held the position of Chaplain of the United States Senate, which has given him a special ministry to government leaders and their families.

Dr. Halverson believes it is possible for a fallen minister to be restored, and he cites the following Scripture passages that assure all believers of forgiveness: 1 John 1:9; Hebrews 10:11–14; and Ephesians 2:8–10; as well as "the whole burden of Scripture, explicitly and implicitly."

Dr. Halverson states that before a fallen minister returns to public ministry, "He should be accountable to a group of sisters and brothers who represent in an official way an established fellowship of believers. He should look to them for direction." The time the fallen minister spends out of the ministry "would depend on the group to whom he is accountable." Dr. Halverson does not feel it would be advantageous for the fallen minister to move to another part of the country, but that decision could best be made by the committee to whom he is accountable.

In response to the question about the length of the waiting period, Dr. Halverson said, "I do not sense any 'rule' about this. But again, it assumes his submission to his counseling group and the opening of circumstances which seem to indicate God's direction."

DR. JACK HAYFORD

In 1969, Dr. Jack Hayford became pastor of The Church On The Way in Van Nuys, California, where he watched the church grow from eighteen members to a congregation numbering in the thousands. His outreach extends to radio, television, and a vast cassette ministry. The author of several books, Dr. Hayford is loved and respected by ministers and lay people throughout the nation.

"Pastor Jack," as his congregation calls him, responded to my questionnaire by sending his new book, *Restoring Fallen Leaders*, which is based on his excellent cassette, "Where Have All the Flowers Gone?" In both messages he shows his love for his two famous televangelist friends whose sin made front-page news for months. But he also demonstrates his deep concern for the cause of Christ. He invited me to find the answers to my questionnaire from his book. Let us begin with his standards for church leadership:

> Spiritual leaders have few privileges but many points of responsibility. Basic qualifications for their role are clearly elaborated in the Word. 1 Timothy 3:1–13, 5:17; Titus 1:5–2:8; and 1 Peter 5:1–11 are foundational in this regard, and

mandate character requirements which must be *proven* and *maintained* if a leader is to be found faithful under Christ's Lordship. Any thoughtful study of these expectations reveals a call *not* to a religious rigidity, but to the development of leaders who accept distinct disciplines and who live in a constancy by those standards.

Facing the issues distilling around the tragedies of fallen spiritual leaders, I see us at a very crucial point. The handling of these issues may well become *THE* issue of our times. *If a surrender to slackness in the requirements of spiritual leadership is conceded now, and if a creeping humanism governs the resolution of this problem,* the authority of Christ and His Word will have been supplanted. Unless an honest confrontation with *all* the Word of God is made *now,* the result will be nothing less than a reduced view of Christ's Lordship—His rule and His will in His Church. . . .

But if these leaders do not own allegiance to *His* standards, ultimately neither will those they lead. Church history verifies this conclusion: inroads of *humanistic opinion* [author's emphasis] in the standards governing the selection and sustaining of the Church's leadership *always* eventuate in the corruption of the whole Church. However painful it may be when it comes to ministering the whole truth of the Word when tragic failure befalls a leader, a high view of the requirements for spiritual leadership must be maintained. This will be done in direct proportion to the degree that a high view of Jesus Himself is maintained.[4]

Pastor Jack concurs with his denomination (Assembly of God) that fallen ministers can be restored after a suitable waiting period during which proper discipline takes place. One of his preferred texts to verify this position is found in Galatians 6:1.

It's a magnificent verse—but as magnanimous as it is in its goal of full recovery, it's also demanding in its directives for restoration; more so than a quick quotation of the verse suggests.

First, an accurate definition of "restore"—its meaning and tense—dictates a radically different stance from that assumed by those demanding a leader's quick return to office. The verb *katartidzo* (restore) means "to mend, to fit or to thoroughly equip," and the tense and mood (present imperative) dictate that the action is intended to be sustained in an ongoing, continual way. The clear command as instructed here might appropriately be paraphrased: *When another person is overtaken in a fault or failure, you who are spiritual people will see to it that you graciously set about the extended task of seeing that person mended and returned to full fitness; doing it in a way that clearly indicates you do not hold yourself as superior to them for their having fallen and all the while remembering your own vulnerability.*

The employment of extended time in restoration is specifically dictated by this oft-quoted verse. Rather than the immediate or quick return which glib usage suggests, the text usually requires precisely the opposite. Opinion has nothing to do with it. The Bible simply says it. . . .

FORGIVENESS AND FRUITFULNESS

The failure of a spiritual leader is a staggeringly painful event in the life of everyone affected by that person. . . .

Forgiveness is instantaneous, but the fruits of repentance take time to grow. The restoration of the scorched fruitage of years of ministry and the repairs of the "cracks" in the character which sinning has exposed cannot be restored in a moment's burst of gracious intent or holy passion.

It is characteristic of most recommendations for quick restoration that too casual an attitude exists concerning the *time* which was involved in leading to the sin, or the time involved in *continuing* the sinful walk *to* which the leader submitted. When grace forgives and then God's Word summons to time for healing and full recovery of the person, it is time to remember: What takes time to break takes time to mend.

Sin isn't the fruit of a moment; neither is restoration. . . .

DISCIPLINE OR PUNISHMENT?

It's a sad fact that many believers see the disciplining of a spiritual leader as an effort on man's part to punish, embarrass, or retaliate. If such unworthy motives have ever been present, they were as unbiblical as the leader's tragic fall. But the requirement of time for restoration is not a punishment— it is an opportunity for another side of "grace" to be shown. . . . It is needful that (1) repentance be humbly manifest and that (2) submission to the restoration process be allowed. The leader needs to declare *both* before those he leads and those who are his peers or leaders in ministry. . . .

The Apostle Paul warned of the price of a spiritual leader's removal from office through failure. "But I discipline my body and bring it into subjection, lest, when I have preached to others, I myself should become disqualified" (1 Cor. 9:27). Every leader has been forewarned by that trumpet call to vigilance sounded in the Word of God.

Failure disqualifies, and requalification takes *time*. . . .

"The discipline of a fallen leader" is not a punishment by others. It is a voluntarily accepted role of one who believes the full teaching of the Word about three things: God's mercy in forgiveness, God's summons to restoration, and the obligation of every spiritual leader to accept the counsel of other leaders in the spirit of submission.

That's what "the discipline of time" is about: healing and mending, not punishment. And the one who accepts that discipline becomes a disciple again, at a fresh point of beginning—forgiven and cleansed, and ready for the process of recovery.

Let us never doubt that by God's Holy Spirit and in accordance with His Word, such a recovery can be complete.[5]

Although Dr. Jack does not specify the amount of time required for restoration, he does offer some guidelines for a restoration committee:

It is not without reason that so many groups recommend or require from one to even four or five years for the recovery of fallen leaders. More and more are accepting a greater responsibility for caring for their fallen: providing transitional financial assistance, expense for counseling, personal support groups, and guidance toward recovery. The strength of this development in the larger Body of Christ is not only in the Christlike care it shows, but in the biblical value being served: Time for restoration—time that is required, but also time that is filled with redemptive action.[6]

DR. DAVID HOCKING

Dr. David Hocking, senior pastor of Calvary Church of Santa Ana, California, is well known for his biblically based expository preaching. He is the Bible teacher on the daily radio series, *The Biola Hour,* the author of several books, as well as a popular Bible conference speaker.

Dr. Hocking defines *restoration* and points out that God holds Christian leaders to a higher standard of behavior.

Restoration (as to definition) refers to believers who, because of sinful actions or life-style that resulted in loss of fellowship/position of service, are now given (by a church or organization) back the relationship/place of leadership that they formerly had. The purpose of church discipline is threefold: (1) the purity of the church (1 Cor. 5:1–13); (2) a warning to others (1 Tim. 5:19–20); (3) the restoration of the disciplined believer (2 Cor. 2:6–8; Philem. 10–12).

In the case of Christian leaders, they are to be examples to other believers (1 Peter 5:3), blameless (without reproach), and characterized by a good reputation/testimony among unbelievers (cf. 1 Tim. 3:2, 7). Their marital commitment is to be without question ("husband of one wife"—a one-woman man—1 Tim. 3:2, 12; Titus 1:6).

All believers who sin against the Lord and others through sexual immorality (adultery, homosexuality, incest, premarital sex, etc.) can be forgiven on the basis of their confession and repentance (Prov. 28:13; Luke 17:3–4; 2 Cor. 7:9–11) and restored to a place of fellowship and service. However, Christian leaders bear a greater responsibility and accountability before the Lord and other believers.

Dr. Hocking further believes that fallen leaders can be restored both to the Lord and to some form of service after repentance and discipline, if certain conditions are met.

Certain factors need to be faced before leaders who have fallen into sexual sin and have repented are allowed to resume their leadership and ministry:
1. Is there evidence of confession and repentance? How much time has transpired since the offense?
2. Is the person still married and giving evidence of fidelity, loyalty, and loving commitment to his spouse?
3. Does the person's public ministry require a greater reluctance to restore his former position? Does it require a restriction upon his future ministry because of

the damaging influence which his example might have been? What effect will this decision have upon the unbelievers whom we are trying to reach for Jesus Christ?

It would seem best in the process of restoration to apply the following principles:

1. The person should not be allowed to exercise his leadership or to minister publicly until a period of time (determined by the church who exercises the discipline) passes by in which the person can be observed and counseled regarding the evidence of repentance.

2. The person should not be restored to the same position of leadership and ministry, lest the public view the decision as compromise or neglect of biblical standards of morality.

3. The person should be encouraged after a period of time has passed to resume leadership and ministry in a limited and different fashion, with humility and a degree of reluctance, ever mindful of the consequences of sin, dependent upon God's grace and forgiveness, obedient to the Word of God, and relying totally upon the power of the Holy Spirit for victory (Ps. 119:9, 11; 1 Cor. 10:13; Gal. 5:16).

While Dr. Hocking did not rule out the possibility of the fallen minister eventually returning to the pulpit, it is quite apparent he believes a man, even after an appropriate discipline period, should come back slowly and under supervision of others. He seems to share the position that once a senior pastor falls, he must be given spiritual oversight by those who can hold him accountable.

DR. JOHN A. HUFFMAN, JR.

As a young pastor at the Key Biscayne Presbyterian Church, God blessed Dr. John Huffman's faithful Bible preaching. During that period he had the opportunity to be a spiritual confidant and to pray with a former United States president who attended Huffman's church during vacations. Later, after serving as the pastor of the First Presbyterian

Church of Pittsburgh, Pennsylvania, he was called to St. Andrew's Presbyterian Church of Newport Beach, California, where he enjoys a growing and effective ministry.

Dr. Huffman indicated that he too has agonized with minister friends whose sin took them through this ordeal.

> I, like you, have walked through some painful pilgrimages with some good men who have, by the circumstances, had to leave the ministry permanently or have found their ministry severely crippled by the Evil One. I have yet to see a person who has not paid a terrible price for this, even if he and his wife have worked it through and found retored relationship with each other.
>
> However, when it is all said and done, I believe that it is unfortunate that we have placed a sexual sin at the top of the pyramid of sins. I accept fully the biblical underlining that all sin is sin and breaks the heart of God. I realize that a sexual sin has a kind of oscillating interplay between the impact it has on one's own individual body and the damage it does to the corporate body. However, we must go to a deeper level, that of Romans 1, that specifically emphasizes the true nature of sin at the root level, which is creature worship instead of Creator worship, with creature worship being the ultimate in idolatry. Paul writes: "Therefore God gave them up in the lusts of their flesh to impurity, to the dishonoring of their bodies among themselves, because they exchanged the truth about God for a lie and worshipped and served the creature rather than the Creator, who is blessed forever! Amen" (Rom. 1:24–25). Then Paul gives that list of sins, covering the whole gamut from abominable sexual sins to envy, strife, deceit, gossip, slander, boastfulness, haughtiness, and disobedience to parents, to name a few. I would hope that the evangelical church would increasingly give as much attention to some of these sins of the flesh instead of encouraging a narcissism in our hero worship that actually sets up our leaders for a fall.

As a Presbyterian, Dr. Huffman is in a denomination that has the advantage of controlling the credentials of a local pastor, and they have an established procedure for such restoration. He did give his opinions that would apply to the whole body of Christ.

I believe that any person involved in adultery needs to deal with this in accountability to a group of his or her peers, who represent structure and definition beyond just a few sympathetic cronies. Whether or not this should be made public, I believe, should be determined in that environment. In most cases, it will end up going public anyway, and it would appear to me that the best course of action is to deal with it clearly, first in the context of those who were wronged and then, if necessary, to the broader public.

I believe how long one should stay out of the ministry should be determined by this accountability group of peers. In our case, it would be the commission of the presbytery and/or ultimately the entire presbytery. I believe a year to three years, depending on the circumstances and what cover-up has gone on. In my view, the lying and deceit are every bit as serious as the sexual sin. In my view, the person who refuses to deal honestly in accountability relationship should not ever be restored to ministry. The person who is transparent before God and his peers can be restored more quickly.

In my opinion, to move to another part of the country doesn't solve anything. It simply displaces the problem. If possible, the people involved should work out the problem closer to home. However, it is very difficult to regain that pastoral leadership in the same congregation where one has previously served.

In reading Dr. Huffman's rather thorough response, I was struck with how his concern for both the fallen minister and the body of Christ was very similar to the concerns of ministers of other denominations. He also showed great concern for the lying and deceit that accompanies sexual sins. And like the others, Dr. Huffman's experience is that even if a fallen leader is eventually restored after a waiting period of a year to three years, life for such a leader will never be the same.

DR. RICHARD LEE

Dr. Lee is the dynamic young pastor of the rapidly growing Rehoboth Baptist Church of Atlanta, Georgia. His popular and expanding television ministry has given him an opportunity to minister to thousands of families each week. At its rate of growth during the past four years, he will be seen in every city in the nation before long. Dr. Lee also has written a number of books.

Dr. Lee believes that under certain circumstances a fallen minister can be restored. He bases his premises on several Scripture passages:

> If we confess our sins, he is faithful and just to forgive us our sins, and to cleanse us from all unrighteousness (1 John 1:9).

> I acknowledged my sin unto thee, and mine iniquity have I not hid. I said, I will confess my transgressions unto the LORD; and thou forgavest the iniquity of my sin (Ps. 32:5).

> Hide thy face from my sins, and blot out all mine iniquities. Create in me a clean heart, O God; and renew a right spirit within me. Cast me not away from thy presence; and take not thy Holy Spirit from me. Restore unto me the joy of thy salvation; and uphold me with thy free Spirit. Then will I teach transgressors thy ways; and sinners shall be converted unto thee (Ps. 51:9–13).

According to Dr. Lee, "The minimum conditions would include a general repentance before God, an acknowledgment of the minister's involvement in the sin, and the seeking of forgiveness from those he had wronged. Also, the timing, method, and forum for 'going public' should be wisely chosen by the counsel and guidance of godly elders."

Regarding the length of the restoration process, he advises, "It would be wise to treat a fallen leader in the same way we would a newborn believer. A new believer would be given time to prove himself, grow in the trials and testings that would come to his life, gain inner strength through his own abilities to stand against temptation, and also be given time once again to demonstrate his trustworthiness that he might gain the confidence of others. In this way he would be considered as having a 'fresh new beginning.' This is not only promised to the new believer, but also to the believer who comes in repentance (1 John 1:9)."

He further suggests, "It would be advisable for the Christian leader to move to a new part of the country before starting a new ministry. But a great deal would depend upon how his repentance took place, and the conditions surrounding it, and the forgiveness on the part of those who were wronged by him."

Dr. Lee believes the waiting period should be less for the person who judges and confesses his own sin than for the person "caught in the act."

If his situation was handled as a new believer (refer to above), the time before he was returned to his ministry would be in relationship to the inner growth and restored confidence given to him by others who are mature in the faith. This process might even include open confession and repentance, a reaffirmation from the church concerning his membership, and an eventual new ordination to the gospel ministry.

Also, I think there would need to be a real evidence of a [sincere] brokenness over sin on his part, and a spirit of genuine remorse over sin's damage to his life and the lives of others. Let me suggest seven areas of remorse that would need to be dealt with. The effect of sin upon:

1.   The heart of God
2.   His own family
3.   The local church in which he ministers
4.   The church of Christ on earth
5.   His own spiritual life
6.   His personal call and ministry
7.   His fellow ministers

Only after he came to a spirit of brokenness over how his sin had affected these areas would I believe he had come to an understanding of the nature and consequence of his fall.

On the other hand, the waiting period for one "caught in the act" might not be as clear. You always question if a person "caught in the act" of sin is experiencing sorrow for the sin itself or sorrow for getting caught.

DR. JOHN MACARTHUR, JR.

Dr. John MacArthur, Jr. has been pastor of Grace Community Church of Sun Valley California for over twenty years, during which time the church has experienced incredible growth, making it one of the largest churches in the Los Angeles area. He is president of the rapidly growing Master's College and Master's Seminary, which emphasize thorough Bible preparation for young people, equipping them for lifetime Christian service. Dr. MacArthur reaches millions of people not only through his books—several of which are best-sellers—but also through his radio ministry, which has earned him the credibility of being considered among the best Bible teachers in the country.

Dr. MacArthur enclosed two articles on this subject and added several thoughts, from which I have distilled the following:

> I have watched with alarm the latest trend in the church. I am shocked at how frequently we are seeing Christian leaders sin grossly, then step back into leadership almost as soon as the publicity dies away. Sadly, Christians don't expect much of their leaders anymore. We are in the midst of a disaster that is certain to have far-reaching consequences. . . .
>
> Gross sin among Christians leaders is epidemic—a symptom that something is seriously wrong with the church. But an even greater problem is lowering biblical standards to accommodate our leaders' sin. The fact that the church is so eager to bring these men right back into leadership indicates a rottenness that goes right to the core.[7]
>
> . . . Cynics are already speculating about who will exposed next, and we can hardly fault them for their skepticism.
>
> The current state of leadership in the church is similar to what Chaucer described in *The Canterbury Tales* six hundred years ago when he wrote: "If gold should rust, what will iron do? For is a priest be foul in whom we trust, no wonder that the common man should rust." Chaucer further described the clergy of his day as manured shepherds trying to clean the sheep. That imagery is perfect.
>
> Today's church faces the same tragic dilemma. The sad fact is that some—perhaps a majority—of the most visible religious leaders of our day are utterly disqualified from spiritual leadership. Yet they purport to speak for God, and their words can be very convincing.[8]

Conservative Christians have for most of this century focused on the battle for doctrinal purity. It is right that we have. But we are losing a battle for moral purity. The worst defeats now seem to be occurring among our most visible leaders. The church cannot lower the standards to accommodate them. It should hold it higher so purity can be regained. If we lose here, we have utterly failed, no matter how orthodox our confession of faith. We can't win if we compromise the biblical standard.

We must recognize that leadership in the church cannot be entered into lightly. The overarching requirement of a leader is that he be above reproach (1 Tim. 3:2, 10; Titus 1:7). That is a very difficult requirement, and not everyone can meet it.

Some kinds of sin irreparably shatter a man's reputation and disqualify him forever—because he can no longer be above reproach. Even Paul, man of God that he was, said he feared such a possibility. First Corinthians 9:27 says, "I buffet my body and make it my slave, lest possibly, after I have preached to others, I myself should be disqualified."

Obviously Paul has sexual immorality in view when referring to the body. In 1 Corinthians 6:18 he says fornication is a sin against the body. It was almost as if he put sexual sin in a category of its own. Certainly it disqualified a man from church leadership. First Timothy 3:2 demands that elders be one-woman men.

Where did we get the idea that a year's leave of absence can restore integrity to a man who has squandered his reputation and destroyed people's trust? Certainly not from the Bible. Trust forfeited is not so easily regained. Once purity in sacrificed, the ability to lead by example is gone forever.[9]

Sexual sin *is* singular in its effects on those who fall to it. Scripture clearly recognizes this. Read 1 Corinthians 6:18–20 and Proverbs 6:32–33, which clearly indicate that the effects of sexual sin are unique in the way they bring a lasting reproach. First Corinthians 9:27 indicates that misuse of the body (sexual sin must be included) disqualifies a man from preaching.

By acknowledging that, I am in no way teaching that sexual sin is morally worse than, say, anger or avarice. Nor do I believe it is the only sin that may permanently cripple one's ability to lead. Any sin that scandalizes the church would have this effect. Especially in the case of an internationally know leader, hideous or scandalous sin leaves a reproach that cannot be blotted out. The persistent memory of betrayal made public leaves such a man unable to stand blameless before people and lead them spiritually (cf. 1 Tim. 2:1–2). Those are the tragic consequences of sin.

It's true that no one is perfect. All of us—including me—fail the Lord and sin against him. Still, it is one thing to fail in a moment of anger and lose one's temper, or stumble in weakness and say something careless or unkind. To compromise with regard to sexual morality and have one's sin be known to the world is another matter because of the lasting reproach that inevitably accompanies such sin.

If a man becomes drunk and loses his leg in an automobile accident, his sin can be forgiven, he can be restored to fellowship, but nothing will give him his leg back. The consequence of his sin will be borne for the rest of his life. So it is with the disgrace of one who sins sexually (Prov. 6:33).[10]

DR. ROSS RHOADS

After many successful years in evangelistic work, Dr. Ross Rhoads accepted a call to Calvary Church of Charlotte, North Carolina, in 1972. During the last eighteen years the church has experienced phenomenal growth and has recently completed the building of an extensive complex. Dr. Rhoads is loved for his biblically based preaching and warm, sensitive spirit of compassion.

Dr. Rhoads believes that while "money problems" and in some cases "bad personality traits or evil dispositions" should also be dealt with as sin when they become apparent in ministers, "sexual sins seem more wicked since they are so visible" when exposed. Like almost all the others, he views sexual or moral sins, against which the Bible warns us many times (see Gal. 5:16–21), as more serious for ministers than other sins.

After the minister's sincere repentance, which should not be "a public-relations venture" but an event experienced within the church family, Dr. Rhoads believes the minister should proceed to spiritual restoration, reconciliation with his wife and family, and restoration to some form of service.

"This may not involve an identical leadership position, but certainly there is some opportunity for service" for those experienced ministers who have sinned and been spiritually restored after a suitable time period. After all, Dr. Rhoads reminds us, "Time heals." And while it is probably advisable that the minister move to another part of the country for a new ministry, he should not rush back into leadership. "I am amazed at the brief time period after which some have returned. Too soon is erring, I believe." He does not set a specific waiting period but believes the issue should be handled on an individual basis. He suggests that "the drawback time should vary with the depth of feeling and recognition of personal shame." Each person should be dealt with in "tenderness and sensitivity."

Like many of the leaders polled for this survey, Pastor Rhoads has clearly been influenced by personal experience with ministers who have fallen. He ministered in the city where for months the Jim Bakker scandals occupied the front page of the local newspaper. "It appears that confession in the traditional sense has become a public-relations venture," he noted. "This error should not 'go public.'" Personal recognition and repentance (after cessation of the sinful activity plus sorrow for the sin) are understandable, he indicated, but we as believers "should cover sin" that brings reproach to the cause of Christ. "I do not mean we should cover up sin. It, of course, must be dealt with by responsible officials within the church but not in the secular press."

Pastor Rhoads's point (not mentioned by the other respondents) is both biblical and relevant. Both the Old and New Testaments state that "love covers a multitude of sins" (Prov. 10:12; 1 Peter 4:8). We need to expose unrepentant sin today, but that exposure, wherever possible, should be confined to the officials of the church. We do not need to distribute more ammunition to those who blaspheme our Lord and his church as the result of the sins of the few.

DR. CHARLES SWINDOLL

"Chuck" Swindoll, as he is known by his vast radio audience, may be the most popular preacher in the country today. He is pastor of the First Evangelical Free Church of Fullerton, California. *Insights for Living,* his popular radio series, has brought help and spiritual healing to millions. Dr. Swindoll has written several best-selling books and has a unique ability to apply biblical principles to the everyday problems of life.

Dr. Swindoll did not return the poll I sent him, but we did discuss the problem personally. We met at a banquet in Los Angeles, immediately after the fall of a highly successful young pastor was announced in the national press. I was a member of the pastoral staff at the time. In fact, just the day before, I had preached to his great congregation immediately after the deacons read his resignation—probably the most difficult preaching experience of my life. As we discussed the moral tragedy that both of us have watched become an epidemic in the church today, I asked Chuck if he had ever known of a Christian leader who had been restored to a ministry equal to the one he had at the time of his fall. He replied, "I have given this considerable thought of late and cannot think of one person, either in the Bible or in life, who survived the exposure of a repeated sexual sin and was restored to the same level of ministry he had previously." I received the distinct impression that night that although he believed in forgiveness, repentance, and renewed service, Dr. Swindoll was convinced that the "polluted priest" could not simply return to his former level of leadership, if ever.

Later Dr. Swindoll aired on his radio program a carefully written letter sent to a friend who had voiced his frustration with fallen Christian leaders who had "climbed back into the spotlight." Like most leaders already cited, Dr. Swindoll believes that Scripture anathematizes sexual sins, for they carry with them other deceptive sins that eventually hurt many people.

One of Swindoll's unique contributions to this study is his conviction that when a Christian leader lives a double life over a period of time—that is, moral in public and immoral in private—he reveals "a deep-seated character flaw." Thus, while he can be forgiven, his character flaw may keep him from being trusted with high-visibility Christian leadership.

On the radio Dr. Swindoll explained,

> The character flaws which led to those extended and deceptive acts of sensuality may very well restrict such individuals from the public service they once knew. Not because they have not repented ... but because this can scandalize the body of Christ if they come back before the public to enjoy all the privileges and rights that once were theirs. It asks too much of those who were deceived and offended to expect them to say, "I forgive you," and then quietly step aside while the newly forgiven brother or sister moves back into a highly visible position before the general public. ... Severe and tragic consequences follow severe and tragic sins. ... Flawed character breeds distrust. ...
>
> Being granted the privilege of public leadership and ministry carries with it the tenuous yet essential presence of power. In Christian service that power is incredibly influential and can be used for selfish purposes, all the while appearing gracious. The temptation to deceive is especially strong in handling such power, thus the constant need for accountability, self-restraint, and discipline.[11]

He then pointed out that the person who surrenders to this temptation has broken a sacred trust. This, of course, violates 1 Timothy 3:1–7 in that the minister has not lived "above reproach." Therefore he is disqualified from leadership. The duration of that hiatus from ministry was not specified, but Dr. Swindoll made it clear that he did not favor an early return—if one would be made at all.

Dr. Swindoll also commented about the demanding attitude of some fallen leaders who insist on a return to public ministry as their right, regardless of what others think.

... There is too little said today about a broken and a contrite spirit. The forgiven sinner of today often expects, or dare I say, demands more than he or she should. Scripture calls this presumption. A broken and a contrite heart is not presumptuous and entertains no expectations. ... A presumptuous spirit usually reveals itself in an aggressive desire to return to a platform to public ministry. When that desire isn't granted, those being restrained can easily present themselves as the pathetic victim of others' judgment. I find that response manipulative and not a little bit disturbing. What concerns me most about this whole scenario is the absence of abject submission to God and utter humility before others. ..."[12]

SUMMARY

The responses of these Christian leaders probably represent the most typical positions on this subject among Bible-believing ministers today. All agree, as we would expect, that fallen leaders need first to repent and work diligently to save their marriages; any future form of service depends on a firm reconciliation with his wife and family. They all believe that such a fallen servant can be forgiven and that God can use him in some capacity.

In other areas, their perspectives differ, primarily on the subject of whether the person's restoration to Christian service could indeed include an eventual return to the pastoral ministry. Two men, Dr. Jerry Falwell and Dr. Criswell, believe he should never be restored as a pastor. Dr. John MacArthur and Dr. Chuck Swindoll seem to agree, particularly if the sin was practiced over a period of time; and if the fallen minister did return to the pulpit, it would not be the equivalent of his former ministry.

The others contend that the fallen minister should be allowed to anticipate a return to a public preaching ministry, but only after adequate discipline and time spent proving his moral and spiritual readiness. All condemn a speedy return to public ministry, and most warn against the danger to

Christianity of a casual attitude toward immorality. Most considered sexual sins greater than other sins, and several identified them as "sins against the body" that should involve church discipline.

Leaders who felt a fallen minister could return to leadership offered various perspectives about the length of the waiting period. The leaders agreed that each case should be handled individually, weighing the extent of the sin and the deceptions that were practiced. Several mentioned the need to ascertain the genuineness of the repentance before restoration is considered. None suggested less than two years for consummated adultery, and some would extend the period to five years, depending on the circumstances. Again, all respondents believed the fallen minister should "prove" himself worthy of such trust. Several, however, would agree with John MacArthur that 'in the case of an internationally know leader, hideous or scandalous sin leaves a reproach that cannot be blotted out. The persistent memory of betrayal made public leaves such a man unable to stand blameless before people and lead them spiritually (cf. 1 Tim. 3:1–2). Those are the tragic consequences of sin."

All respondents agreed that such tragedies will continue to occur and that we serve the cause of Christ in discussing the matter openly. It is my hope that this book and others like it will help to warn ministers of the high cost of moral breakdown and strengthen them for the hours of temptation that they may face.

CHAPTER 10

A Personal Perspective

*I*t is always risky to offer an opinion about a controversial subject after others already have expressed their convictions. I offer mine here, not as the final word, but as a carefully drawn conclusion after several years of consideration. I have discussed the issues privately with scores of fellow ministers and Christian leaders, finding no consensus and not expecting one to be formed.

THREE CRITICAL ISSUES

Before offering my personal viewpoint, let me review three questions that I feel need to be addressed when considering a minister for restoration to ministry.

What Is the Minister's True Character?

Sexual sins are so grievous and so contrary to the ministry of the indwelling Holy Spirit and to everything taught by the Bible that they must be considered as weakness-of-character sins. No one ever commits "just" a sexual sin; the situation almost always involves deceit. Sometimes an elaborate web of lies is spun, first to initiate a relationship and then, of course, to cover it up. Adulterers sometimes will cheat, steal, or even kill to conceal their sin. King David is a classic example. He lusted after Bathsheba, committed adultery, then lied and constructed an elaborate method of deception to cover his sin, finally murdering her husband. If the "sweet psalmist of Israel" could stoop to such sin after adultery, how can we trust any adulterer?

People who become involved in sexual sin reveal a serious character flaw. Admittedly, the immoral deed may occur at a time of low spiritual ebb or as the result of overwork or in the throes of a mid-life crisis, but at that moment, it reflects a serious character weakness. And that makes restoration to ministry risky.

In situations of sexual sin, one size does not fit all. Instead, every case must be evaluated individually. Any restoration to ministry must be based not just on the sex act alone but on what that act reveals about the minister's character. Did his affair include many acts of deception? Did he initiate the affair? Did he tell his wife about it? Did he terminate the illicit relationship at his own initiative? Is he repentant? Did he reveal deep hypocrisy, preaching boldly about the biblical view of marriage and sexuality during the period of time he was involved in an affair? Did he come to the church board to confess his sin or did they have to approach him? What was his response to confrontation by the church board or elders? Does he accept personal responsibility for his sin or does he blame others? Is he responsive to the church's discipline of him? Is he willing to throw himself on the mercy of God and his peers for the possibility of restoration to ministry? Is he willing to subordinate himself to the will and Word of God? Does he insist on an immediate return to the ministry?

How Long Did the Sexual Sin Go On?

A second concern in considering a minister for restoration to ministry is the length of time he was involved in an illicit sexual relationship and the number of times the relationship was consummated. Obviously, the minister who has one sexual encounter should be treated differently from the minister who has dozens of encounters. Similarly, the minister who has a two-month affair is treated differently from one whose affair lasted for seven years. The length of a minister's involvement in sexual sin often signals the depth of the sin.

In several of the cases with which I am familiar, the minister couldn't live with the weight of sin on him, and thus his return to God followed soon after his fall. In one such case, the man's sin covered only one month of a ten-year ministry. A case could be made for the strength of his true character and spiritual life in that he was able to judge his own sin and "flee from it." Admittedly, his infidelity disclosed severe weaknesses, but the fact that he could not perpetuate a sin of passion tells us something positive about his true character and spiritual life.

We need to remember that ministers have a spiritual advantage: "Judgment Day" arrives every Saturday night! Only a cold, desensitized Christian can prepare to face a congregation with unconfessed sin in his heart and still expect the Holy Spirit to empower him on Sunday morning.

A minister who commits a sexual sin usually feels remorse, repents in secret, and experiences great difficulty preaching or teaching after he sins. He pleads the blood of Christ for forgiveness, and because God is faithful, the minister may even see fruit in the hearts of his congregation.

If, however, he falls again, he may find it easier to continue in the sin. Over time he may become indifferent to his immoral behavior and even to the Holy Spirit. When his sin is finally exposed, such a person may have gone beyond restoration because he is beyond the call of the Spirit.

One man I know, perpetrating his sin over one-third of his time in ministry, slowly stifled the convicting voice of the Holy Spirit and did not end his illicit relationship until he was exposed. Evidently he had committed "the sin that leads to death," a reference to the protracted practice of sin (1 John 5:16). This minister died suddenly and tragically only a few months after his exposure.

How Many People Were Involved?

In considering whether or not to restore an adulterous minister to public ministry, we should take into account the number of people involved in his sexual sin. Did the minister have sexual involvement with only one person or did he have several affairs?

How many people is too many? Some say one. Others have reinstated ministers who have had affairs with several people. If a poll were taken, many Bible-believing ministers would not permit restoration to ministry for even one moral misstep. However, an increasing number of churches are beginning to lean toward restoring a fallen minister to ministry after a one-person affair (if, of course, adequate signs of repentance are manifested and if the affair was not a lengthy one). However, if the minister has been sexually involved with two women, his chances of restoration to ministry decline rapidly, and involvement with three women suggests a dangerous pattern that would seem to disallow restoration.

CHRISTIAN RESTORATION

I believe that on the basis of the character studies reviewed in chapter 8 and the teaching in Galatians 6:1— "Brothers, if someone is caught in a sin, you who are spiritual should restore him gently"—fallen ministers can under certain circumstances be restored to public ministry. The passage in Galatians specifically teaches restoration after sin. It doesn't specify what sin or what Christians, but it also doesn't exclude ministers taken in adultery. This text is aimed at restoring Christians who are living in sin at the time the restoration process is to begin taking place. Most of the conscientious ministers that I have dealt with are in a stronger position than that, having already ceased their immorality, repented voluntarily, and renewed their relationship to the Lord.

Since the Scripture gives no specific command prohibiting a fallen minister from returning to pastoral or public ministry, I would conclude that if over a period of time a minister faithfully meets the appropriate requirements for restoration, then he *gradually* should be allowed to assume whatever ministry the Holy Spirit opens to him—provided he submits to some form of accountability for the rest of his life. A fallen minister can bring to his restored ministry a new brokenness and humility that God can use in other broken lives. In several cases, a fallen minister is an example to the believers (1 Cor. 10:11) of the high price that must be paid for adultery. But even at best, I do not believe his ministry will ever be the same.

All Christians are sinners. If only perfect vessels or those whose entire ministry was "above reproach" were allowed to continue preaching, there wouldn't be enough qualified ministers to fill all the churches in one state—much less the fifty states and the rest of the world. As reprehensible as it is for a minister to commit adultery, I see no reason to identify it as the one sin for which he cannot be restored—particularly in light of the many Bible characters whose lives we have reviewed. How could a holy God honor an adulterer and murderer like King David? Because he remembers our confessed sins no more (Heb. 10:17). Is adultery the unpardonable sin? Of course not! God forgives adulterous ministers and supplies their needs—if they truly seek his forgiveness and are willing to pay the cost of restoration.

RESTORATION SHOULD BE DETERMINED
BY THE FALL

While I believe that the Scripture teaches that a fallen minister *can be* restored to ministry, I do not believe all fallen ministers *should be* restored. All ministers are different, and circumstances surrounding their sexual sin vary radically. Each minister should be evaluated individually in the three areas outlined at the beginning of this chapter. The evaluation should be done by a group of spiritually mature men who have known the minister well for many years.

First, the minister's *true character* should be examined. How did he handle his sin? If he was involved in pervasive deception in an attempt to disguise his sexual sin, then he's not ready for restoration to ministry. If he has shown no clear evidence of a deep and sincere repentance, then he's not ready for restoration. If he refuses to accept responsibility for his sin and to submit to authority that will assure further accountability, then he's not ready for restoration.

On the other hand, if the fallen minister sincerely confesses and repents of his sin and readily submits to the discipline of the restoration committee, then he has made a step toward restoration. If he becomes aware of his own vulnerability to sexual sin and establishes spiritual safeguards and a system of regular accountability, then he has taken another step toward restoration.

Second, the *length of time* the minister was involved in sexual sin should be considered. If the minister was carrying on an affair for several years, indicating an increased dullness to the Spirit's conviction of sin, then he's not ready for restoration to ministry and possibly never will be. He will need time to reprove his trustworthiness and moral purity. The longer he was involved in sexual sin, the longer it will take him to regain his spiritual strength and establish necessary trust.

However, if the minister voluntarily stopped his sexual involvement after a very short period of time, he may be revealing his sensitivity to his own sin. That already is a positive step toward restoration. That doesn't mean that his adultery is treated lightly by any means. But it may indicate that his basic character is stronger than his temporary character flaw.

Third, the *number of women* with whom the minister has been involved should be considered. In my opinion, ministers involved with several sexual partners should never again return to Christian leadership or a prominent public ministry again. The man who has engaged in several affairs proves he is too weak in this area to be granted spiritual leadership. As a man it is difficult for him to walk a holy life. He doesn't need the added temptation pressures that almost all ministers face.

One minister was investigated by his denominational leaders because of reported infidelity. They discovered three cases in his present church, became suspicious, investigated his previous ministry, and uncovered four others. Such persistent sin disqualifies him as a trusted leader. I believe he may find other employment in the Lord's work, but never as a minister.

THE WAY OF THE TRANSGRESSOR
SHOULD BE HARD
(PROVERBS 13:15)

I believe that sexual sin should not be dealt with lightly. Sexual immorality is one of the most grievous sins a minister can commit. Next to heresy, denying the Lord, and murder, I can't think of any greater betrayal of trust, for it involves so many people: the Lord, the man's wife and family, the other woman and her family, his congregation, the body of Christ, and the lost people he would have reached for Christ, etc.

When a minister desecrates his position by sexual indiscretion, he can never again regain his former status of integrity. God may use him in some form of ministry after a significant waiting period, but I do not believe he will ever achieve the heights he may have reached if he had not sinned sexually. He will always be a former adulterer. Even forgiveness will not change that in the eyes of man.

The consequence of sexual sin should never be easy. Some people, wanting not to cause a stir in the church, treat the sin too lightly. Let's say, for example, that a minister has an affair with a married woman in his congregation, and the woman's husband finds out about the affair. Thinking he's protecting his family and doing the church a favor, the husband doesn't tell the church board or elders about what has happened. Instead, he quietly transfers the couples' membership to another church.

Overlooking the minister's involvement does not help the minister or the church. The husband should have told the official board of the church. When the board learns that the minister has been involved in sexual immorality, it should realize that other women could become additional victims. Sin is subtle. If a person gets away with it too easily the first time, he may sense little restraint the next time.

The board should confront the minister and advise his wife in order to assure future moral accountability. Public exposure obviously makes the road to restoration to ministry more difficult. However, Galatians 6:1 indicates that the purpose of confrontation is restoration, not just to fellowship but to service.

The board should then remove the minister from that ministry, thereby protecting the women of the congregation and giving God an opportunity to deal with him, insuring that he will not be so vulnerable when future temptation strikes.

The minister needs to prove himself again in order to be qualified for the ministry.

Rebuilding trust and respect takes time—usually more time than it took the minister to prove himself worthy of the ministry originally. I've asked many godly women how they would react if their minister were involved in sexual sin. First I asked them: "If your pastor—whom you loved and admired—committed adultery, confessed his sin, and was restored to his wife, would you forgive him?" Almost every woman replied, "Yes!" Then I added, "If he genuinely repented, stayed out of ministry for one or two years, and was recommissioned to the ministry by a group of his peers, would you and your family attend his church and raise your children under his ministry?" Over 90 percent said, "No." Most uttered that negative emphatically! Trust takes time.

A Christian counselor whose assistance was needed in a case of adultery mistakenly thought that because the minister had "repented" and the woman's family had left the church, the other issues would resolve themselves. He felt no need to expose the minister's sin to anyone else, not even the church board or the minister's wife. How wrong he was. Because the minister escaped too easily, he repeated his error two years later. But this time his fall occasioned a public disgrace that hurt many people—and the cause of Christ.

One particular case illustrates that the way of the trangressor is hard, even if he follows the right path after his sin. A minister repented of an adulterous relationship that extended over a period of several weeks. Life was agony for him as the Holy Spirit wrenched him with guilt. Finally he repented and labored to reestablish his relationship to the Lord and his wife. A trusted elder provided accountability against the possibility of repetition. God richly blessed the fallen minister for many years afterward. Several churches were developed from his growing congregation, many souls were won to Christ, millions of dollars sent to the mission field, and a number of missionary candidates and future ministers were called into God's service through his faithful teaching. Obviously, God used this good man after he repented of his sin.

Almost a decade later the details of his fall leaked out. He and his family were humiliated, and he resigned in disgrace from the church where he had been mightily used of God. He voluntarily stayed out of ministry for one year, then was recommissioned to the service of the Lord after being investigated by a group of his peers. Today he is back in ministry as a copastor with many preaching opportunities. No one seeing his life could say there is not a high price for sin—even for sins repented of and forsaken.

RESTORATION IS RISKY BUSINESS

An evangelist told me this story of his friend, a minister of a large, missionary-minded church. When the evangelist heard that his friend had left his wife and three children to live in another state with another woman, the evangelist could hardly bear it. His friend would not answer his calls or letters, so finally the evangelist drove to the place where his friend now lived and searched the city until he found him. When his fallen friend opened the door, they stared at each other. Finally, the friend burst into tears.

Eventually, because of the loving concern of the evangelist, the friend repented and returned to his family. The evangelist arranged for the friend to speak to his former congregation. After the evangelist gave the message at a Sunday evening service, he asked the congregation to remain in the sanctuary. Then he called their former minister to the platform. The minister confessed his sin, asked their forgiveness, and resigned, acknowledging he was no longer worthy to be their minister. There was not a dry eye in the church. Many embraced him and tearfully promised to pray for him. The church proceeded to call another minister and has put that tragedy behind it as it continues to grow.

Over a year later another pastor from a distant city, a friend of both the minister and the evangelist, invited the fallen minister to join his staff as an associate minister with limited public duties. Three years later he was called to a church out West, where he pastored successfully for three years. And then he had another affair. This time, of course, there will be no restoration to ministry.

You are probably aware that one televangelist disregarded the waiting period required by his denomination and returned in three months, even though he had been, in essence, defrocked. His action caused several of his associates to give up their ministerial credentials rather than leave his organization. Whether he will rebuild his ministry to what it once was remains to be seen. His advertised gross income is currently running less than half of what it had been before his sin. Given his extraordinary gifts, he may someday rebuild it fully, but I doubt it. Life for him will never be the same.

Other renewal attempts have been more successful. I personally am aware of three ministers who are doing extremely well, and another friend claims he knows of seven who are still faithfully serving God. Several have gone into related ministries that do not involve public preaching or pastoring; all have learned their lesson and are now playing it straight—I think.

None of them, however, is experiencing the ministry he would have enjoyed if he had never committed sexual sin. These men may be forgiven and restored to public ministry, but for them, neither life nor the ministry will ever again be the same. Only eternity will "wipe away all tears from their eyes."

There is no question in my mind that the best hope for a fallen leader to return to ministry is official restoration by a responsible restoration committee and a recommissioning service by a church. How to do that will be the subject of the next chapter.

CHAPTER 11

A Model for Restoring Fallen Ministers

All fallen ministers need forgiveness and spiritual rebuilding. According to the good news of the gospel, not only does God forgive sinners when they repent, but "the blood of Jesus Christ his Son cleanses us from all sin" (1 John 1:7 NKJV). The word *cleanse* appears in the continuing action in the Greek, meaning that Christ's blood keeps on cleansing us, that we as Christians can have constant cleansing—every time we repent and confess our sins.

Galatians 6:1 reminds us that the church is responsible for the restoration process. And we should remember that restoration is a process, not an instantaneous experience like forgiveness. The restoration process should begin by helping the minister rebuild his spiritual life, his marriage and family, and his fellowship in the body of Christ. Ideally that rebuilding should extend to restoration to ministry.

The following suggestions are intended to serve as a basic model that can be adapted or modified by a local restoration committee.

THE RESTORATION COMMITTEE

We have already clarified in chapter 6 that a fallen leader needs a restoration committee with which to work. This is particularly true for a senior minister or highly visible person in a church that lacks a denominational procedure.

It is usually helpful if the church where the sin occurred initiates the restoration committee. First, they know the fallen minister most deeply. Second, they can provide a unifying force by informing the congregation that a group of spiritual leaders will responsibly nurture the former minister and his family. Third, when it serves in love, this committee can form a buffer between the fallen leader and the church, assuring a positive relationship between them as they go their separate ways to serve the Lord.

If the local church is too disorganized or too angry to structure a proper restoration process, a committee of local ministers who know and preferably have worked with the fallen minister should be asked to serve. All members of the committee should have the best interests of the church, the fallen minister, and the body of Christ in view.

Committee members should be selected very carefully. The members must be spiritually mature people who can deal effectively with a weighty responsibility. The committee members should be gifted with discernment, compassion, and wisdom as they approach the various areas included within the process. For instance, one member should be particularly qualified to assess the minister's spiritual re-building, another his marriage, and still another his moral conduct. Because of the very sensitive nature of their work, all members should be people of high integrity, people who pledge to keep every discussion and all facts confidential. That is why I recommend that the committee should be limited to three or five members.

The committee members should be objective, loving, and supportive of the process of restoration to ministry. This is no place for a person who has previously expressed animosity toward the minister, or opposes the principle of restoration.

One restoration committee that turned into an inquisition was headed by a man who opposed restoration to public ministry for any fallen minister. The tragic turn of these men against their former minister should have been predictable. For in addition to a chairman, who opposed restoration to ministry, the committee contained two staff members who used their position to retaliate. Ironically, after the committee was abandoned in futility, the chairman changed his mind and wrote a letter of apology to his former minister and friend. By then, however, the damage had already been done. Whereas the minister brought great shame to his church, the committee brought dishonor to the cause of Christ through the unloving and unkind treatment to which it subjected the minister and his family. Had the minister not earned the respect of so many fellow ministers during his years of service in that city, it is doubtful that he would ever have been restored to public ministry. The restoration committee established such an antagonistic tone within the church that even the calling of a new minister did not settle the church for quite some time.

STEPS TO RESTORATION TO MINISTRY

The function of the restoration committee should be to help rebuild the fallen minister's spiritual life and marriage, measure his progress, hold him accountable, demonstrate love, and address related issues, like finding a job. After the committee has been selected and a chairperson has been appointed, the committee should meet with the fallen minister regularly to focus on the following areas of concern.

Step One: Assure Genuine Repentance

Sorrow for sin is not always the same as genuine repentance. Whenever secret sins are publicized for all to see, sorrow on the part of the sinner inevitably follows—for two reasons. Secret sins somehow look different, even to the sinner himself, when they are made public. In addition, he is sorry when he gets caught because of the terrible effect private sin has on all those he loves.

Consequently, the sorrow, brokenness, and tears that any sinner manifests when he is exposed may not reflect true repentance. The fallen one may not be trying to deceive others, but he may be deluding himself. In his book *Rebuilding Your Broken World,* Gordon MacDonald describes true repentance clearly.

> *Repentance* is a Middle Eastern word. It describes the act of turning around when people realize that they have been going in the wrong direction. It was most likely used in nonreligious settings, such as when a traveler asked directions of someone who knew the countryside and was informed that he'd taken the wrong road and was moving away and not toward his destination. In such a conversation, it would be appropriate for the one to say to the other, "You're going to have to repent and head for that road."
>
> And so the practical word *repent* became useful to describe a moral and spiritual act also. Used by Older Testament prophets, then John the Baptizer, Jesus, and finally the apostles, it meant to change the direction in which the heart was inclined.
>
> John the Baptizer made repentance the theme of every public talk. He spoke of a repentance that took place first in the heart and then in the moral performance patterns of the individual. The latter he called "the fruits of repentance."
>
> When repentant men and women stepped forward and said, "What kind of fruits are you talking about?" he would speak to them about their clear concern for the poor, their renunciation of violence, and their commitment to justice. These things, he said, would clearly indicate that something in the freed-up heart was different.[1]

Very simply, true repentance is effected by a change of heart and will. We exchange our will and desires for the will of God in that arena of life. In the area of morality, we renounce our naturally promiscuous, carnal desires for God's moral standard—commitment to marriage—with no exceptions. Anything short of that is not valid repentance.

Again I must caution (and it grieves me to do so because so many current fallen leaders are my personal friends) that sexual sinners can be clever liars and deceivers, having diligently practiced cover-up schemes for months or years. Consequently, they can't automatically be trusted to tell the whole truth.

All fallen ministers know that the first step on the way back to leadership is repentance. So together with the shame of exposure, the pain caused to themselves and their family, and the overpowering desire to return to ministry, they can be so convincing in expressions of sorrow that they may satisfy everyone that they have genuinely repented—including themselves. A restoration committee should carefully determine whether the repentance is genuine or merely an expression of sorrow for being caught. The following signs usually signal *genuine* repentance.

Uninhibited confession. Whenever a confronted sex offender admits only to the offenses with which he is charged, I get suspicious that he is holding something back. Conversely, when a person truly faces his sin, his confession is often an explosive thing. Sexual sins, unless they have been practiced so long that the person's conscience is "seared as with a hot iron," are so vile that they produce an enormous pressure of guilt, and confession becomes the natural release valve for that pressure. Confronting a truly repentant minister is like pricking a balloon with a pin—the minister bursts into confession, acknowledging many other sins unknown to the confronter.

That is particularly true of a sincere minister whose sin

violates everything he knows about God's moral law, his own conscience, and his marriage vows. It is not uncommon for him secretly to yearn for exposure, for the guilt becomes immeasurably heavy. Yet he can't bring himself to break off the relationship. Consequently, when confronted, he not only confesses to his infidelity but also discloses other deeds known only to him and his adulterous partner.

Although the fallen minister does not have to confess everything to everyone, genuine repentance will include divulging everything to someone (in strictest confidence, of course). Either that person or the person who heard the minister's first confession should report to the restoration committee that he did indeed make a full confession. He does not need to repeat all the details of that confession—just the assurance that it was genuine. It would be a gross betrayal of trust for anyone on that committee to share whatever confidential information they are privy to with anyone else.

Several years ago I was moved to reach out to a confessed sexual sinner and help him find a nonpublic ministry during his restoration process because during our first interview he confided "everything." In some cases, he acknowledged things I didn't need to know—or so I thought. But this turned out to be providential. The spirit of antagonism toward him was so strong that I received several phone calls from angry Christians in his former church, wanting me to know all about this man. As it turned out, no one told me anything new—he had already confessed it all. That is usually a sign of true repentance. Today this man is back in public ministry and is still practicing accountability.

The acceptance of all blame. The repentance of one well known fallen minister who has been restored to public ministry is a good example of how to right a bad situation. By the time his sin was finally exposed, he had already voluntarily confessed everything to three trusted elders and his wife. In addition, he accepted all the blame for his sin. In every public interview this minister gives, the other woman is rarely mentioned. Like the repentant prodigal, this minister readily announces, "I have sinned against heaven and in your sight." It is not surprising his confession and eventual restoration was so readily accepted by the Christian community.

I am suspicious about the depth of repentance in the minister who protests, "It was the woman who caused me to sin" or "I was under enormous pressure at the time." That is like saying, "God's grace was *not* sufficient for me." All fallen ministers have no one to blame but themselves, and until they accept that fact, they are not ready for restoration to any form of Christian service.

Contrast that with the response of one fallen friend in whose repentance I have great confidence. As we conversed, his wife became agitated as she described the unloving attacks on him by the restoration committee, which used its position to further humiliate him. He tenderly touched her hand and cautioned, "Honey, it's really not their fault. If I had not sinned in the first place, they would never have had an opportunity to treat me that way." Such genuine repentance can lead the way to restoration to ministry.

Spontaneous humility. When a minister is exposed publicly for immoral conduct, he normally is swept with brokenness and humility—as the Bible identifies it, "a broken and contrite spirit." How long that spirit of humility lasts will often indicate the depth of repentance.

One minister maintained a humble spirit for a few months. During that period he acted in the best interest of the church—resigning, acknowledging his sin, and leaving town for several weeks. But remaining out of the spotlight and away from the instruments of power he previously enjoyed gnawed at him until he began to formulate self-justifying reasons for a return to the public ministry. No longer was he interested in restoration by an appointed group of his peers. He rejected the advice of minister friends, who all warned against a hasty return to the ministry. His lack of humility made even his closest friends doubt the sincerity of his repentance—and vote against his restoration.

Contrast that with the man who moved to a nearby town and spent much time humbly restoring his marriage and his relationship to God. His peers were so impressed with the genuineness of his repentance that one of them spontaneously started a movement to restore him to ministry. Every minister who was asked to participate in a restoration committee for him accepted. When they were confronted by his humble spirit, the Holy Spirit witnessed to their hearts that the man had truly repented.

Total resubmission to Christ. Fallen ministers know about surrender. Almost all of the fallen ministers cited in this book were totally surrendered to God during their early years of ministry. They had preached about surrendering our bodies as living sacrifices and probably had seen many people answer that call to the Lord's will. But after a sexual fall, a minister needs to experience that surrender in a fresh, new way.

I have found that fallen ministers, especially those who before their fall had been associated with large, growing ministries, often envision their restoration including a call to another church comparable in size to their former churches. These ministers often are not prepared to surrender this vision, to submit to a different plan for their lives. They fail to realize two important problems: first, he and his family may not be ready for that kind of ministry; and second, churches may not be ready to call a minister who has had a sexual fall.

Occasionally I receive letters from pulpit committee chairmen asking that I recommend a pastor for their church. So far none have responded after I suggested a fallen friend whose spirit, discipline, and restoration have prepared him to resume a pulpit ministry. In fact, sometimes fallen ministers have been rejected by churches twelve times smaller than the one they left.

The fallen minister must adopt a new goal: surrender of his total life to God as a willing servant to do *anything* God requires. Submission to God for a preaching ministry or leadership position is bargaining with God, not surrender. In essence, one is saying, "I'll serve you if you give me my old position back or one like it." A true servant implicitly obeys every directive of his master. Peter was reluctant to accept our Lord's challenge to "feed my sheep" partly because he had lost confidence in himself. The fallen leader who has betrayed the Lord by his conduct should humbly fear that he may again bring reproach to the cause of Christ, and thus his spirit of obedience and subservience ought to be heightened as he approaches restoration.

No demands. Everyone is alienated by the fallen leader who forcefully demands the right to continue in the spotlight. That was apparent with the well-publicized televangelists who considered a slap on the wrist sufficient to inaugurate a return to their ministries. Former ministers sometimes do not seem to realize the significance of their moral failure.

A truly repentant servant simply wants to serve God. He will sweep the floor, knock on doors, drive a Sunday-school bus—anything to get back into his Lord's employ. One fallen pastor, whose administrating skills were apparent in his large congregation, turned down a job with an electronics firm that would pay him an annual salary of $80,000—if he would commit himself to the company for three years. Even though he had no job and needed an income, the thought of not serving the Lord for three more years made the high salary unattractive. Later he accepted a job as a business administrator of a large church that paid him half the salary. But, he explained, "At least it's a start back in the Lord's work."

Instead of making demands of God and the Christian

community, the repentant fallen minister will have to do what he has preached so often to others: be faithful in serving God today, whatever the opportunity, and trust him to provide other doors of service tomorrow. In practicing this kind of submission, the minister will make it clear that his restoration to ministry is the work of God, not of his own determined will.

Step Two: Help Rebuild the Minister's Spiritual Life

No one commits adultery while in a close, vibrant relationship with God. Consequently, like any sinner, the fallen minister will have to spend serious time growing in grace and knowledge of the Lord and relearning to walk in the Spirit and not in the flesh.

Ideally a person from the restoration committee will meet weekly with the minister for Bible study and prayer as well as for giving other assignments to strengthen the minister's spiritual life. That should include daily personal Bible reading, at least one Scripture verse to memorize weekly, a written Bible study, and a book-reading assignment. A fallen leader who is not willing to submit to rehabilitation of his spiritual life is not ready for restoration to ministry.

If someone outside the restoration committee is better qualified to maintain this relationship with the minister, then the committee can appoint that person to work with him. The appointed person should report to the committee regularly about the the minister's spiritual progress and about recommendations concerning restoration.

Step Three: Help Rebuild the Minister's Marriage

Most churches with which I am familiar pay to give the minister and his wife biblical counseling with a Christian psychologist or experienced marriage counselor. The couple needs an impartial person to diagnose the problems that contributed to the infidelity and to help them work through the hurt. Counseling should include a tactful examination of their sex life, their spiritual relationship, and other areas of their marriage, including finances, child raising, and conflict resolution. The counselor, then, should submit regular reports to the committee, outlining the couple's progress.

Again I must warn that such a counselor should be carefully selected. He or she should be an experienced marriage counselor who uses biblical concepts in therapy.

If at all possible, the committee should arrange for this counseling to be done at a retreat center for an intense period of time, perhaps two or three weeks. This way the couple can spend protracted time together and work consistently on their relationship with the help of a spiritual, experienced counselor. If a problem with sexual inadequacy has led to the infidelity, it will come to light. It is imperative that an intimate sexual relationship between them be established.

Special attention should be given to helping the wife truly forgive her husband. Then she can summon God's grace to restore their relationship. Otherwise their marriage will be in jeopardy. The husband will need help to understand that it will take time and many expressions of love for his wife to learn to trust him again.

During the first few months of the restoration process, the husband should develop the habit of calling his wife frequently to let her know where he is, particularly if there is an unexpected change in his schedule. Wives of fallen leaders want to believe in their husbands again, and the more they hear from them, the easier it is to develop that trust. The telephone is a handy instrument to solidify close communication. A wise husband voluntarily submits to such accountability to his wife. She should be able to look her husband in the eye and ask him if he is being faithful to her and if he has been attracted to another woman. She also should feel free to acknowledge her uneasiness about any woman's aggressive conduct. Anything the couple can do to promote open communication between them is helpful.

After the couple has been in counseling for several months, someone on the restoration committee should interview the wife of the fallen minister to see how they are doing in rebuilding their relationship. Because she knows him better than anyone else does, she is in a unique position to express her perspective about whether or not she feels he is ready to be restored to some form of Christian service.

Step Four: Help the Minister Find Work

Sooner or later the fallen leader will have to earn money and provide for his family. Even though I have recommended a financial severance in proportion to the man's length of service to that ministry, eventually it will run out. For that reason the fallen minister should find some means of support. It will not be as satisfying as Christian service— nothing really is once one has experienced full-time work in the Lord's vineyard. But it will help occupy his time and thoughts and give him a sense of being productive until the Lord opens a door to Christian service. I know of ministers who have temporarily gone into real estate, sales, administration, motivational lecturing, teaching, etc.

Step Five: Establish a Waiting Period

The length of time a fallen leader must stay out of public ministry should be established by the committee itself unless the church instructs it otherwise. As we have seen, almost all responsible Christians expect the minister to spend a reasonable time out of the public eye, concentrating on his personal life and family before he even can be considered for restoration to public ministry. The shortest period I am familiar with for adultery is two years, and it could go as high as five, depending on the factors already mentioned.

The waiting period is primarily a proving time. It should require as much time as necessary to assure that the minister is rehabilitated spiritually and morally before assuming the role of spiritual leader and teacher of the Word of God. Two factors must be kept in mind: first, the minister's willingness to salvage his talents, experience, and training; and second, the minister's assurance to the church and community that he will not be involved in further sexual sin.

The celebrated case of a well-known minister who was forced to resign from a national ministry due to exposure after only one year in the restoration process is somewhat misleading. While the church itself publicly restored him at the end of that year, he had already repented of his sin, told his wife, and voluntarily put himself under the accountability of three trusted friends who were experienced Christian leaders—over a year before his fall became public. Consequently, the actual time of his restoration period was at least two years.

Step Six: Convene the Restoration Service

Once the committee establishes that the fallen minister has been properly rehabilitated, it should recommend that the church proceed with a public restoration or recommissioning service. The ideal church to call this public service should be the minister's former pastorate, where the sin occurred. If this is not possible, then the church where he is currently an active member may initiate such a service, or a neighboring minister can offer this opportunity.

The restoration service should focus not on the minister's sin but on the restoration process. A few members of the committee may wish to speak at the service, assuring the congregation of the fallen minister's confession and the rebuilding of his spiritual life and marriage. Then a new charge can be given to the minister, asking him to make a public commitment to holiness and ministry.

On the strength of this public recommission by a

responsible body of believers, a fallen minister is restored to ministry. Not only will this service make it easier for some church to consider him to be its pastor, but it also will be a rich blessing to the church, especially if it is the one where the sexual sin occurred. The service will have a healing effect on the congregation, particularly between people who have become seriously divided during the sad experience.

Step Seven: Consider the Open Door

Once the restoration service is complete, the minister is now ready to serve the Lord on a full-time basis. By this time, the minister ideally has been involved in nonpublic Christian service, under the supervision of the restoration committee. For example, he may have been active in visitation, evangelism, a bus ministry, administration, or other support services. Now he is available for Sunday school and Bible teaching, prayer services, weddings, and funerals. If the minister desires, he may preach occasionally. Personally, I would rather not see him become a senior minister for at least one more year unless it is in a small church that cannot find anyone else to accept its invitation. God alone knows the depth of his rehabilitation and can lead accordingly. Our Lord made it clear that he is the God of the open door (see Rev. 3:8). The same Lord who called and led the minister before his sexual sin can direct and use him now.

Currently I have observed the following "open doors" used by God to bring restored ministers back into ministry.

An associate pastorate. A fallen minister usually has pastor friends who still believe in him and his potential service for our Lord. If a staff need arises, they will invite him to share in the many facets of pastoral ministry again. This may last from one to several years until he receives a call to become the pastor of a church.

Church planting. A restored minister with a mission could begin a new church. It is never easy to break ground for a new ministry, but thousands of churches have grown out of home Bible studies, and many others are the result of door-to-door evangelism. But unless the fallen minister is recommissioned and sponsored by the church where the sin occurred, he should not start a new church in the city where he had his affair.

"Difficult" ministry. Some churches, due to the makeup of the old or changing neighborhood, are considered "difficult churches." I don't believe a church can be labeled "difficult," but I do recognize communities that find it hard to attract ministers. A congregation may call a restored minister and give him a chance to rebuild its once-great ministry. If he is a gifted preacher whose repentance is considered genuine, this may be worth the risk. Biblical preaching and soul winning are still the major keys to the growth of over 95 percent of the flourishing churches in the nation. This is one way in which a "difficult church" could call an outstanding preacher and experienced pastor to its pulpit.

Para-church ministry. Mature and proven administrators who can lead an organization into the next level of its development are always in demand. A restored minister may find a place in such a ministry.

Pastoral ministry. My personal poll of godly women indicated that 90 percent said they would not attend such a man's church. However, because of the pastor who recommends him or because of the fallen man's pastoral gifts, some churches may give him a call, particularly if he is currently serving successfully on a church staff.

Step Eight: Establish Ongoing Voluntary Accountability

A fallen minister is wise to keep himself under accountability. That is, some trusted friends have his permission to invade his personal life at will, holding him accountable for his behavior. Upon hearing or seeing anything in his conduct that causes suspicion, they will confront him with a request for the truth. Even without provocation they are permitted to ask, while looking him straight in the eye, "Friend, have you kept yourself morally pure since we last met?" When they hear an affirmative reply, they may add, "Have you had any close calls lately?" At least six of my friends know that when they pick me up at the airport or whenever we meet, I am likely to ask those questions. Two are former homosexuals, four are former adulterers. Part of my reason for doing this is to reinforce their will. When confronted with temptation—and they surely will be—I want them to think, "But the next time I see my friend Tim, he will ask me if I am still clean." The anticipation of that question may reduce temptation to manageable size.

I recommend that at least three people be given such voluntary accountability rights: the minister's wife, a spiritual leader from the restoration committee, and a Christian friend in leadership.

Summary

Because of the nature of human frailty, there will be some failures in such a process. Even so, I believe it is worth the risk when proper accountability has been established to minimize the possibility of a recurrence. Most fallen ministers I know learned a major lesson from their tragedy. They cannot trust their "flesh" because they are certain to face again the temptation to fall into sexual sin, they must always be on their guard. By following the above procedures and accountability, even a weak brother can become "strong in the Lord and in the power of his might" so that his talents and years of experience can be used for years to come in advancing God's kingdom.

CHAPTER 12

How One Church Restored Its Minister

*T*he story you are about to read is true, the names are withheld purposely to protect the fallen leader, now restored. Because books have a shelf life of several decades, I have chosen to withhold the name of this well-known minister who was officially restored to public ministry after a suitable period of discipline and rehabilitation. Currently, he is serving as pastor of a historic church in a metropolitan center.

The minister's fall into sexual sin after almost twenty-five years of Christian service surprised many people. He was not the flamboyant leader of a personality cult whose fall is often greeted with "I have been expecting something like this." In his case, the whole Christian community was saddened.

We are talking about a model Christian leader, properly prepared, happily married, and very "successful." Yet at a low period in his spiritual and emotional life, he entered into an illicit relationship with a Christian woman, an experience neither of them ever dreamed they could commit.

Describing his sin on a Christian radio program, the

minister pointed out something from which all of us can profit. Quoting someone else, he warned, "An unguarded strength becomes a double weakness." He thought, like many of us, that his love for his Lord and his wife made him immune to moral temptation. Not so! And he will bear the defeat of that brief period of his life as long as he lives.

But there is another lesson to be gained. After experiencing the enormous guilt and pain of exposure (pain described by this man as the greatest of his entire life), one may be restored *if* he is genuinely repentant and *if* responsible Christian grace is extended to him. As we have seen, under such circumstances a fallen Christian leader can be restored to public ministry.

This was the case for the man I am describing. In the Lord's time, he may again productively serve our Lord as one called to preach the Word. Consequently I do not use his name here because I want him to be remembered decades from now for additional contributions to the kingdom of God, not for his brief sexual fall, which is already four years old. If God can't remember his confessed sin against him any more, neither should the church, now that we have ample reason to believe his fall will not be repeated.

THREE KEYS TO THIS MODEL OF RESTORATION

Just as every ministerial fall is unique, so is the restoration—if it occurs at all. This particular model features three key ingredients, all of which must be present before an appropriate recommissioning service can be conducted.

The Church

The church this minister had served is a large congregation of loving, forgiving people who are grounded in the Word of God. Although they maintain high moral standards for all their leaders, they also practice Christian forgiveness. In addition, they are appreciative of the twelve years of faithful service their former minister invested in them.

The New Pastor

The present pastor, whom I have never met, must be a mature man, spiritually and psychologically. He led the elders and church leaders in working with the former minister, keeping the best interest of the former minister and his family in mind as the leaders endeavored to restore him to spiritual productivity. I don't know whether or not the new pastor was a friend of the fallen minister, but the new pastor could not have acted more lovingly if he had been.

Personally, I don't deem it possible for a church to restore a fallen minister unless the new pastor is willing to extend his heartfelt and enthusiastic support. But such an effort is risky! If a new pastor tries to restore a fallen, former minister without the leading of the Holy Spirit and the support of the congregation, he could be initiating a divisive action that might harm his own ministry. That would particularly be true if he tried to move too quickly and without adequate preparation. On the other hand, if the new pastor follows the leading of the Spirit, the restoration of the fallen minister can be a unifying and gratifying experience.

The Fallen Minister

The minister in this story demonstrated all the signs of genuine repentance. He sincerely confessed his sin before it was discovered; he told his wife everything; he voluntarily disclosed the details to three older and highly respected Christian leaders, making himself accountable to them. When his sin was made public, he withdrew himself from all public ministry and dedicated himself full time to restoring his spiritual life and his marriage.

The minister made no excuses for his conduct, did not

blame the equally guilty other party, but accepted all the responsibility for his actions. He did not demand that the Christian community reinstate him into ministry but rather resisted some well-meaning friends who tried to press him back into service too quickly. Throughout it all he has manifested a truly humble spirit, the kind of attitude the Lord loves to bless. The "damage control" put into practice in this situation was so exemplary that, under the circumstances, it caused the least possible discredit to Christ's church.

HOW THE CHURCH PROCEEDED

The following information was gleaned from a cassette recording graciously sent by the church being discussed. Through it I was able to hear the entire recommissioning service that was conducted before a congregation of twelve hundred people.

When the elders first heard the rumors of their former minister's fall, they were in the midst of a two-day planning session. The chairman of the board of elders immediately called the former minister to verify the disturbing news. Through his tears the minister acknowledged his sin on the phone to the chairman and later to the entire group. These elders were immediately moved to prayer. "What can we do to help?" they inquired.

At the next elders' meeting, the new pastor led them in a Bible study on the subject of restoration, based on Galatians 6. Since the former minister had left their church to enter a para-church ministry, their church was his only real church home. When they asked if he was willing to submit to their watchful care and discipline, he immediately agreed and identified the three men with whom he was already working. A subcommittee of the elders was established to act as a liaison between the three men and the fallen minister, who met with the subcommittee several times and submitted a written report to them each month during the disciplinary period.

Finally, after much prayer and discussion within the entire group of elders, they voted unanimously to proceed with a public service to restore him officially to ministry. This decision was based on their studied belief that "he was rightly related to God and his family, had manifested genuine repentance, and had agreed to submit to ongoing accountability." They were also impressed that the Holy Spirit had given the fallen minister a "new message of hope" to the body of Christ. Safeguards were established, and he was encouraged to accept small opportunities to speak. These have led to others as churches have responded to his humble spirit and faithful teaching of the Word.

THE PUBLIC SERVICE

The recommissioning service was exceptionally inspirational. The present pastor led with an excellent message on the purpose of church discipline from Matthew 18 and Hebrews 12, clarifying that discipline was not intended to destroy fallen Christians but to restore them. He pointed out that "discipline produces holiness." He then defined mercy as "God not giving us what we deserve" and grace as "God giving us what we do not deserve." The service included brief messages by some of those who had worked with the former minister during his restoration period, and then the former minister himself was invited to speak. It was truly moving!

Finally the elders offered special prayer on behalf of the former minister, and he was recommissioned to the ministry with the official approval of that body of believers. The spirit of rejoicing in the church confirmed that the elders did indeed voice the spirit of the congregation.

For a period of some thirteen months after this recommissioning service, the newly restored minister preached wherever he was invited as he waited on God to open doors.

Although he never expected to return to the pastorate, a metropolitan church that itself had sustained an internal struggle over leadership contacted him to be their pastor. He was forthright with them about his past, but they persisted. "If you're a broken person, then we've got a place for you, because we're a congregation of broken people."

After extensive prayer, the restored minister and his wife felt led to accept this congregation of approximately three hundred people. If he continues to walk humbly before God and ministers the Word faithfully to this rather young congregation, the church will be used of the Holy Spirit to "bind up the brokenhearted, to comfort those who mourn, and to proclaim the year of the Lord's favor" while building up the believers in their faith.

NOTES

CHAPTER 1

1. Phillip Chalk, "A Jim and Tammy Tale in Dallas," *Dallas Magazine* (September 1988): 39–84.
2. "How Common is Pastoral Indiscretion?" *Leadership* IX, no. 1 (Winter 1988): 12.
3. Ibid., 13.
4. Ibid., 12.

CHAPTER 3

1. Richard Exley, *Perils of Power: Immorality in the Ministry* (Tulsa, Oklahoma: Honor Books, 1988), 40.
2. Ibid., 39.
3. Bill Hybels, "The Character Crisis," May 24, 1987, Willow Creek Community Church, Seeds Tape Ministry, Tape No. M8721.
4. Exley, 53–55.
5. Ibid., 62–63.
6. Hybels, "The Character Crisis."
7. "The War Within: An Anatomy of Lust," *Leadership* III, no. 4 (Fall 1982): 41–42.

CHAPTER 4

1. Joyce Price, "Fidelity: Soon to Be Extinct In Marriages?" Washington *Times,* 18 June 1989.

CHAPTER 5

1. Richard Exley, *Perils of Power,* 34–37, 128–29.

CHAPTER 9

1. Assemblies of God Constitution, (Article IX), 133, 134, 136, 138, 139.

2. Edward G. Dobson, "Should a Fallen Leader Be Restored?" *Fundamentalist Journal* (May 1989): 12, 61.

3. Ibid., 61.

4. Jack W. Hayford, *Restoring Fallen Leaders* (Ventura, California: Regal Books, 1988), 18–21.

5. Ibid., 25–26, 35–38, 40–41, 44, 48.

6. Ibid., 53.

7. John MacArthur, "Should Fallen Leaders Be Restored?" *Masterpiece* (Fall 1988): 4.

8. John MacArthur, "Manured Shepherds and Clean Sheep," *Masterpiece* (Fall 1988): 3.

9. MacArthur, "Should Fallen Leaders Be Restored?" 4.

10. John MacArthur, Personal correspondence.

11. Charles Swindoll, *Insights for Living*, radio broadcast.

12. John MacArthur, radio broadcast.

CHAPTER 11

1. Gordon MacDonald, *Rebuilding Your Broken World* (Nashville: Oliver-Nelson,) 156.